Living the
MOMENT

Living the MOMENT

A True Story

My dearest friend Edith
We stood together in prayer for
Craig and Lisa and the Father heard us.
Now they stand together with Jesus,
waiting for us to join them.

From my heart
Léonie

LÉONIE EDWARDS May 2013

AuthorHouse™
1663 Liberty Drive
Bloomington, IN 47403
www.authorhouse.com
Phone: 1-800-839-8640

Published by AuthorHouse 04/22/2013

ISBN: 978-1-4817-8682-9 (sc)
ISBN: 978-1-4817-8091-9 (hc)
ISBN: 978-1-4817-8683-6 (e)

This book is printed on acid-free paper.

I dedicate this book to

my beloved husband

Ian

who held my hand as we

walked this road together

Acknowledgements

Our special thanks go to Sister Debbie from Hospice East Rand, whose love and care for our son we will never forget. The support she gave to Ian and me was more than we could ever have asked for. Hospice East Rand played a major role in helping us make Craig as comfortable as possible in his final days. Winnie, Craig's devoted caregiver, we will always remember with love; also Merriam, who stood in for Winnie a number of times. Our thanks go to Martha, our faithful housekeeper of over twenty years, who was also there for Craig. We are grateful, too, to those dedicated neurosurgeons, radiation oncologists, and medical staff at the hospital where Craig received his treatment. Their commitment to saving lives became part of our support system, bringing constant hope to our plight. To Pastor André and Pat, and Benoni Baptist Church, for their prayers and friendship during Craig's last few months, we thank you with all our hearts. Thanks to Pastor Gary and Angela for their love and spiritual support. To our precious children: Doug and Lindy; Debbie; Brian and Nicky, and my brother, Tony, whose love and assistance never failed us: you are the best—all of you. We dearly appreciate our brother and sister-in-law, Rob and Lynne for coming so far to be with us in our time of mourning; and my sisters, Karen and Jane, across the ocean, for their moral support. From me to my husband Ian, to whom I have dedicated this book: thank you. Thanks to the many friends who visited throughout this trying time, bringing meals and words of hope and love. To all our wonderful friends globally, who emailed messages and sent cards of encouragement, your names are far too many to mention on this page, but they are engrained in our hearts. Our eternal gratitude goes to the hundreds of people who prayed for Craig over four difficult years. God bless you all. And most importantly, thanks to our Lord and Saviour, Jesus Christ, who has never left our sides.

Introduction

Like any other tragic occurrence, the diagnosis of a brain tumour impacts not only the life of the victim, but the lives of those around him. I knew a man who fought a courageous battle with such an affliction. His name was Craig, and he was my son. Even though he was an adult who'd been out of the house for years, there was never a morning when I awoke without him on my mind, never a plan in my own life that didn't centre on his well-being, never a prayer that did not include him. I am a mother. I believe that is what mothers do when their children are in trouble, even if their children are adults.

Craig was the third of my four children. I think that most mothers love their children equally, yet differently. Each one of my children is a testimony of faith, hope, and love.

I was very young when my eldest child was born into circumstances that made life extremely difficult. When he was six years old his father and I were divorced, and he went to live with his father when he was twelve. Years of heartache followed, but in his early adulthood, all that was lost between my son and me was redeemed.

My little girl was born in a time of financial need. She arrived with a club foot, only six toe-nails, webbed fingers, and one and a half fingers missing—a devastating blow for a young mother of only twenty, or indeed for any mother. There was no money for medical expenses, yet she received the necessary treatment throughout the first sixteen years of her life. There were many miracles, with much joy between the anxious moments. She was sometimes shunned at school, but she was an overcomer, and she showed me a thing or two about learning to smile through the tears. Today she has two beautiful daughters of her own. She taught them at a young age not to pick their noses because "look what happens to your fingers if you do!"

And my youngest son—ah yes, he was the one who told people that he liked being the youngest in the family because "the little one gets the most love!" That's not true, but when he was small, he obviously thought it was. But you have to let go, even of the littlest one, and he has taken a few hard knocks in his life. There've been times when I wanted to take it all away from him and bear the pain for him, but we can't do that, even as I couldn't take the pain away from Craig.

Perhaps you're reading this book because you're facing a similar tribulation. If so, then I would encourage you to take heart and allow God to walk this rocky road with you. I can't tell you it won't be difficult. I can't tell you it's all going to be okay. I can't tell you that your prayers will be answered the way you would like them to be. What I can tell you is that if you put your hope and trust in Him, He will enable you to cope with whatever lies ahead.

That's what I believe, anyway.

My favourite photo—Craig aged 18 and me

With Dad (Ian) on Craig's 34th birthday

Chapter 1

In 2008, on the eleventh day of the eleventh month, at 11:00 a.m., Craig had his first major brain operation. It lasted six hours. Hospital rules, as we understood them at that time, were that no visitor was allowed onto the premises outside visiting hours. Much later on, I was to learn ways of bypassing that one, but that day we accepted that we had no alternative but to wait until 3:00 p.m. before we could see our son. It was hell.

Ian went to work that morning, and I sat in our sun lounge, gazing blankly at the garden. Summer flowers had started blooming, and all the trees were green, different shades of beautiful, peaceful greens, but the person who sat looking at them was not at peace. A stranger was about to cut my boy's head open, and it scared me to the core.

It was Poppy Day in Commonwealth countries, the Day of Remembrance, the day they commemorated those soldiers who died in the First World War. Hostilities formally ended at the eleventh hour of the eleventh day of the eleventh month of 1918, with the German signing of the armistice, exactly ninety years ago. Would this be a day of remembrance for me too? I had to banish the thought. It was winter in England, but here, in South Africa, the summer was filled with a promise of good things to come. That thought was better.

Who could have imagined that this would happen to us? The cliché tells us that bad things happen only to "other people", but it never tells us who the other people are. This was to be the beginning of a series of bad dreams that exist only in the minds of moviemakers. And yet there would inevitably come those magic moments when one tumbles out of bed with the rising sun to the inviting flavour of hot coffee and pancakes and a breeze of resilient air, bringing hope to the soul. Thank God for the morning.

Craig Ian Edwards was born on 30 October 1971 in what was then Rhodesia. He had a pretty normal childhood and grew up incessantly fighting with his younger brother, which I was told was a healthy relationship, though who decided that I do not know. He had an older brother and sister as well, but the age gap between the two pairs was around ten years, so in his early years, he related more to his younger brother Brian.

When Craig was thirteen, we immigrated to South Africa. After passing his matric exams, he left school, completed eighteen months of national service in the South African Army of the day, did an apprenticeship, and got a job. There were girlfriends along the way, but Craig never married, nor did he have children of his own. When he reached his late twenties, he moved in with his current girlfriend, who had children, the youngest of whom lived with them.

I've chosen to write a large part of this book in diary form because much of it is extracted from emails that I sent to friends and family over a four-year period, relating the events and progress made by our son, who suddenly, at the age of thirty-six, was diagnosed with a serious brain tumour. It changed his life, affecting many other lives as well. A healthy person all his life, with an almost cynical approach towards doctors, Craig wouldn't even take a headache tablet, maintaining that any headache he may have would disappear naturally in its own time. Most of them did, but not this one.

When researching a medical condition on the Internet, I firmly contend that we should not assume that the named affliction, or its prescribed treatment, is exactly what we have or need. One disease can have many offshoots, making self-diagnosis potentially dangerous. Typically, that's what Craig did when his initial headaches began to worsen. He visited a doctor who prescribed medication. Craig immediately consulted the Internet and found that this was the treatment used for cluster headaches, which are deemed to produce the worst pain a human being can suffer. Based on that information, he concluded that cluster headaches were what he had. He read on the Internet that this was an incurable, but non-life-threatening condition and promptly faced the so-called fact that he'd have to live with it. The symptoms of cluster headaches were evidently the same as the headaches that Craig was experiencing.

I remember well the conversation my husband, Ian, and I had with him a few days before he finally decided to seek further medical advice. He had popped in at our home after work one evening, having driven some forty kilometres from work on the motorway, with a literally blinding headache. He was managing a printer ink shop in Cresta, Johannesburg, and would sometimes come by to drop off cartridges that I had ordered for my office, or he'd bring ink to refill my personal printer cartridges. He was sitting at the dining room table, filling a cartridge, when I noticed that he kept turning his eyes away and shaking his head.

He looked at us and asked, "Do my eyes look funny?"

"No," Ian answered. "Why do you ask?"

"They feel funny," Craig said, removing his glasses and rubbing his eyes. He'd been wearing glasses since he was fifteen, due to short-sightedness, like his father.

"Craig, what's going on?" I asked, "Do you have one of those headaches again?"

"Don't worry about it," he answered.

I raised my voice. "Of course I'm worried about it. In fact I'm getting seriously angry with you!"

He mumbled something about it being his problem, not mine, and carried on filling the cartridge.

"No," I said loudly. "It is *our* problem, mine and Dad's. We've been telling you for ages to do something about these headaches. One of these days you'll drop dead; *then* tell us it's not our problem!"

Ian nudged me, shaking his head and mouthing that I should calm down, but I was adamant.

"So what are you going to do about it?"

Craig looked up from what he was doing. "I did go and see *your* doctor and he gave me some pills that didn't work."

"Yes, I know you saw our doctor, but I have no doubt he told you to come back if the headaches didn't improve," I emphasised.

Craig shrugged. "You know I don't have medical aid, so I can't afford to go running around from one doctor to another."

"Oh right," I said sarcastically. "So you're going to sit back and let this kill you!"

"Rubbish!" he retorted, rubbing his eyes and looking away from what he was doing again. "I'm not a child, you know."

"Well, you're damned well behaving like one! You shouldn't be driving in this condition!"

Craig didn't look at me when he snapped, "What do you expect me to do? How am I supposed to get work? I've gotta make a living, and I don't have money for doctors."

"Craig," I said angrily, "you are starting to infuriate me. Can't you quit being stubborn for once?"

"Come on, Léonie," Ian said after his usual bout of silence, "let's end this conversation now."

But Léonie was on a roll. "No! Why isn't anyone listening to me? And why do you keep moving your head that way?"

"Because my eyesight keeps going."

"What do you mean?" Ian asked.

He looked at us. "Now I see you, now I don't."

"Craig, this is not funny! Tell us what's going on!" I demanded.

"I seem to be losing my sight," he said. "It comes and goes."

"That does it!" I exclaimed, "I'm making an appointment for you to see an eye specialist. If there's something wrong with your eyes, then it's no wonder you're getting headaches."

What I didn't say was that I had an awful feeling this was more than a problem with his eyes. I was recollecting how a few weeks back he'd been groaning about earache. He'd gone and bought some cone shaped ear candles to try and clear them out, explaining that these candles were put into the ear and lit at the other end, which apparently drew out any excess wax and dirt, but to my mind, it was a dubious procedure indeed. I don't think the candle phase lasted long, and Craig hadn't said much more about it since then.

"How much does a specialist charge?" he asked.

"I don't know," I said. "I'll make some enquiries tomorrow."

"Thanks, Mom," he said, handing me the cartridge. "This should work now."

He stood up to leave, and I knew that the first thing he would do when he got into his car would be to light a cigarette. He'd been smoking for years and had no qualms about doing it in front of me, but his father had never seen him with a cigarette. Of course, Ian knew that he smoked. He habitually remarked to me that he could smell it, but Craig was fully aware that Ian hated smoking, and having the greatest respect for his father, he didn't wish to offend him in any way. It wasn't that he didn't respect me, but I was simply jolly old mother, who wouldn't protest. He knew that I'd been a smoker in my younger days, and he therefore assumed that I would tolerate his habit. I did understand that it's not an easy habit to kick, but I hated it as much as Ian did.

"He should stop smoking cigarettes," Ian said, after Craig had gone.

"He can't," I said in Craig's defence. "But if you feel so strongly about it, why don't you tell him?"

"Why don't you?"

"I have, but he doesn't listen to me."

"He should know better," Ian said.

"Well he doesn't."

The next morning, after phoning three ophthalmologists, I managed to secure an urgent appointment for the following day. Craig was thoroughly examined and was found to have severe oedema, or papilledema, on both optic nerves. We were to learn that the optic nerve, whose surface is covered in cerebral spinal fluid to protect the nerve from sudden movement, connects the eye with the brain. If the pressure of the fluid is increased, probably from swelling of the brain, it can compress the optic nerve as it enters the back of the eye. Brain tumours are a common cause of increased pressure of cerebral spinal fluid. Symptoms of papilledema are severe headaches, nausea, vomiting, and in many cases, spasmodic visual blackouts, usually triggered by change in position, such as sudden movement, or coughing, a definite pattern in Craig's case. The ophthalmologist stressed the urgency for Craig to seek further medical attention. Because he wasn't covered for private treatment, he was immediately referred to the eye clinic at a government hospital, which I will refer to henceforth as "The Hospital". Government, or state hospitals in South Africa, make a small charge for treatment, according to one's income. The Hospital is one of the largest medical training centres in South Africa.

It was a relief to know that at last something was being done about Craig's condition, but we had no conception of the long road that lay ahead. As parents, Ian and I were apprehensive, and although I was keen to hear the prognosis, I was secretly very afraid.

I will thank God until the day I die for all the miracles He performed throughout this trying time. I have a personal journal, which is where I write my innermost sentiments. On 6 October 2008, I was expressing my anger towards Craig for not consulting a doctor about his headaches and diminishing eyesight. As I was writing, my eyes focused on the scripture at the bottom of the page, and I decided that this was the Word of God on which I would stand concerning my beloved son and in every other area of my life. I quote from Proverbs 3:5-6 (KJV).

> Trust in the Lord with all thine heart; and lean not unto thine own understanding. In all thy ways acknowledge him, and he shall direct thy paths.

It's easy to trust God in desperate circumstances, but it's also easy to take your focus off Him. I have learned to trust Him implicitly. I do not lean on my own understanding, because most of the time I simply don't have any. I never tried to understand why my son contracted a tumour, and I never questioned God as to what He was doing about it, but I prayed constantly, promising God that no matter what happened to Craig, I would never stop trusting Him. It is only by His grace that I'm able to write this story today.

Chapter 2

Ian and I had booked for a long overdue holiday to the Cape on Sunday, 12 October 2008. It had taken me months, even years, to persuade him that we needed a little holiday on our own, but he's never been particularly enthusiastic about holidays, so I took the initiative and made all the arrangements as soon as he gave the slightest hint of agreeing to go. Now we were confronted with a potential crisis in Craig's life, but the whole family urged us to go ahead with our plans, because Craig had had problems for a while, and our other two sons, Doug and Brian, felt that there wouldn't be any news for at least a week, by which time we'd be back. Craig also wanted us to go, probably because he felt guilty about spoiling our holiday. Not wanting him to stress about it, we elected to go. His appointment at the eye clinic was scheduled for Monday, 13 October.

We rose early on Sunday the twelfth, driving for nine hours, a slightly roundabout route to our first stop at Hogsback in the Eastern Cape mountains, planning to continue our journey on to Knysna the next day. We were preparing for breakfast at 6:00 a.m. when we received a somewhat hysterical call from Craig's partner, Georgie, telling us that he'd been rushed to hospital the previous evening with a massive seizure. A CAT scan had revealed a brain tumour the size of a small orange. When she used the word "cancer", terror flared up within my being.

"No! No! No!" I was shrieking, "This can't be!" I dropped to my knees beside the bed, crying out to God as I had never done before. Ian took the phone and called Doug and Brian, who already knew. They had contacted our daughter Debbie, who lives in England with her family. We were told that Craig was in The Hospital, which is about thirty kilometres from where we all live in Benoni. They said this hospital was exceptionally strict about visiting hours, and that the only time we could visit was between 3:00 p.m. and 5:00 p.m. daily. Later on I was to learn much about that institution—how to cut corners and bypass the system, so to speak. But right then all we knew was that we had to make it to The Hospital before 5:00 p.m. if we wanted to see our son. Ian never speeds, but he was doing a little over the speed limit when traffic police stopped him. I did something I would not have believed I could do. I stretched out my hand to the traffic officer, took his hand, and pleaded with him that this was a life and death situation, apologising for speeding and promising we wouldn't do it again. He nodded and let us go, but it was the look on his face that made me cry. I will never forget it. I would have liked to have found him again and told him that we made it in time.

Finding The Hospital was a navigational feat of note, and negotiating our way around it was an even greater challenge. The massive concrete complex is situated on hilly terrain and comprises various medical training units and student accommodation, the main hospital building being nine storeys high and about 350 metres in length. Doug and Brian had been directing us by cell phone and after one or two wrong turns, we finally reached our destination. The huge underground parking lot was pretty full, because it was visiting hours, but we managed to park reasonably close to the escalators, a spot I came to regard as my space for the next few years. We could have taken one of the elevators, but we were to learn they were not the most reliable form of transport. Neither, in fact, were the escalators, but at least one could climb up those. This, along with my deteriorating hip, was soon to become part of the norm. That day the escalators were working, but I think we ran up them anyway. Up two high floors we went, arriving on the main corridor of the building, which runs the whole length of the fifth floor. The building is divided into five colour-coded blocks. We landed on Green Block, turned left, and rushed down to Blue Block, which is at the far end of the building, up a flight of stairs and left into 456, the neurosurgical ward. The first number, 4, depicts the colour Blue; the second number, 5, the department or ward number; and 6 is the sixth floor. It's a very well thought out system of organisation—once you get to understand it!

Tuesday, 14 October 2008—Email sent to friends and family around the world

Doug, Brian, and their spouses, as well as Craig's partner, had been at the hospital since 3:00 p.m. We found Craig in ICU. He was asleep when we arrived, just twenty minutes before the close of visiting hours. He was heavily sedated to alleviate the pain and was traumatised, but he seemed to know we were there and managed a grunt and a hand squeeze. This morning I phoned, and they told me he was awake and much improved. He was talking and even had breakfast.

There are many people here who are praying for him, and I heard that there's a prayer chain happening in Israel. I praise the Lord for that. This certainly has been a test of my faith, but somehow through it all, I've managed to stay reasonably calm.

We've heard some adverse allegations about state hospitals in this country, but I have to say that in the section where Craig is, conditions are good and he's getting the best attention. He's alone in the ward, which although basic, is clean, and he has a nursing sister with him at all times. There have, however, been some conflicting reports about what will be done for him. Various staff members have different stories. Daily visits are paid by neurosurgeons, between certain hours, which is the only time one can get to speak to them—with a bit of luck! Brian spoke to a neurosurgeon yesterday, but Ian and I haven't been able to get hold of one today. Surgery seems imminent; but *when?* is the question.

We are overwhelmed by all the phone calls, emails, and text messages we've had from many people in the last twenty-four hours. I cannot keep in constant touch with everyone, so please forgive the bulk emails, which apart from keeping you in touch, are my way of keeping a personal journal of Craig's progress. For those of you who have so kindly started prayer chains across the globe, you are welcome to forward my mails to anyone who has taken an interest in our son. We already owe thanks to a number of folks who don't even know us.

Wednesday, 15 October 2008

We saw Craig sitting up and talking, in fact quite cheerful, yesterday afternoon. He had vague recollections of our being there the day before, but had obviously been confused. We told him about the tumour, and he accepted the news well. His vision has deteriorated considerably; he's only able to see shapes, even with his glasses on, but was not unduly perturbed about that. He says that he's sure this will improve once they've operated. I hope he's right.

Ian and I finally managed to talk to a lone neurosurgeon who was roaming around during visiting hours. He told us that until a biopsy is done, there's no way of knowing whether or not the tumour is malignant, which means that the first report we heard when we were in the Cape was unsubstantiated. The CAT scan identified a large tumour in Craig's head, but the nature of such a tumour can be determined only by a biopsy. A CT, or CAT, brain scan is commonly used to detect problems within the skull, such as bleeding, fractures, blood clots, brain tumours, enlarged cavities, diseases, and malformations. CAT (Computer Axial Tomography) scans produce two-dimensional images, but show only horizontal pictures. It is necessary for an MRI (Magnetic Resonance Imaging) scan to be done before the biopsy is performed, because this will be used to examine the brain anatomy and present a picture of the brain's structure. MRIs also monitor the growth of brain tumours and assess the effects of damage to the brain. The surgeon told us that the MRI would be done as soon as possible, but he wasn't able to say exactly when. Most of the neurosurgeons are presently in Cape Town on conference. They are due back tomorrow, but there are cases that are more serious than Craig's, so those will be dealt with first. In the meantime Craig has been stabilized with medication, and we were told that a few more days won't hurt him.

Although his status can't be verified right now, the surgeon we saw said there were various possibilities. The tumour may have been there for years. Craig may even have been born with it. If it's the type of tumour the surgeon suspects, it's quite common and not invasive. He doesn't seem to think it's malignant, but it will have to be removed anyway. He explained that "benign" means a non-cancerous abnormal growth, whereas "malignant" means it is formed from invasive cancer cells. A foreign body in one's head can be very dangerous, malignant or not. He added that benign tumours can turn malignant at a later stage, so whichever way one looks at it, this monster has to go.

Craig is enjoying the hospital food, which is amusing, because it's rather Africanised. I was amazed when I saw him getting stuck into a greasy vet koek (that's a doughy thing fried in oil and filled with curried mincemeat and in this case, cabbage). It was quite bizarre to watch him, considering that he'd been admitted to hospital the night before, in a very serious condition. One of the neurosurgeons actually told me that they were surprised to see him alive the following morning. The way he looks now is more than a miracle. Poor fellow, he wants to reimburse us for the money we lost due to our non-holiday.

Our youngest son, Brian, will be having a back operation on the twenty-eighth of this month. He's had a lot of trouble; two discs in his upper spine will be replaced. He also has symptoms that do not directly relate to these two discs, but they're hoping to be able to fix everything at once.

Thursday, 16 October 2008—Email

What a time this has been! The days are long and the nights are even longer. Negative thoughts tend to run amok in my mind, and it becomes difficult to obliterate them when nothing constructive is happening.

Somebody showed Craig his scans yesterday, and he was quite disturbed. I haven't seen them and I don't want to. He pretended he was okay with it, but he obviously was not. He later admitted he was scared, although he was still laughing, joking, and trying to make light of everything. One would not have thought there was much wrong with him. Georgie shaved him; it was an odd feeling knowing that we were in an ICU and here was a man eating expensive Swiss chocolates, drinking Coke, and shaving. He was whinging about not being able to have a bath, but there are no baths or showers in the ICU because people are usually too ill to bath. Craig was so wide awake that he hated the bed bath scenario, to say nothing of the toilet facilities. However, his good cheer prevailed, despite the underlying tension amongst the family. Brian didn't visit that day, and the only one there who wasn't bothered was good old level-headed Doug. I went home feeling that the devil was pounding my head, filling it with ghastly thoughts. I ended up breaking down for the first time during this ordeal. I had cried when I initially heard the news, but that didn't compare with last night. Brian phoned, and Ian made me speak to him, which was a good thing. He talked me through it all in a practical manner, making me feel a lot better.

Some time ago he had made plans to go to Durban this coming weekend to ride his bike in the 100 km race from Pietermaritzburg to Durban, but wasn't sure if he'd be able to do it because of his back. He and his girlfriend, Nicky, had booked a timeshare for a week and had determined to go for their little holiday, even if he wasn't able to ride in the race. However, Craig became ill, and they decided to cancel the whole trip. We persuaded them to go, although I didn't think Brian would ride in the race. Last night, after calming me down, he told me that riding did not affect his upper back, and he was sure he could still do it.

I was anxious, but then he said, "Mom, I want to ride the race for Craig."

How could I try to talk him out of it? When he visited Craig, he mentioned this. Craig's reply was that if he was still around this time next year, they could ride the race together. I'm so proud of those boys. Our kids are really pulling together. Debbie phoned Craig on Brian's cell phone in the ward yesterday. I know how hard it must be for her on the other side of the ocean. We are blessed to have such a family as this.

Friday, 17 October 2008

Although I'd calmed down, I won't pretend that I enjoyed the rest of that evening, after speaking to Brian. We went to bed, and I couldn't sleep at all, so I got up and sat in the lounge in the dark until 2:00 a.m., talking quietly to God and crying. I went back to bed, so tired that I thought I would surely pass out, but I never did, and finally arose at 6:00 a.m.

This time my day started well. I made tea for Ian and myself, and then picked up an old King James Bible that used to belong to my Dad. Here's what I read:

> I will bring the blind by a way that they knew not; I will lead them in paths they have not known: I will make darkness light before them, and crooked things straight. These things will I do unto them, and not forsake them. (Isaiah 42:16)

Bearing in mind that Craig's eyesight is not at all good, this was a blessed start to my day. When we saw him, he was looking quite perky. He'd been moved out of ICU into a high care unit, with seven others in his ward, and he looked healthier than all of them. He even got out of bed, and Brian helped him to the loo. His face was no longer swollen, and his eyes looked good; in fact, he was able to read, if not too well. The hospital has basics only, hence no radio or TV, so he was chuffed with the tiny battery operated radio that Doug sent for him. It didn't take him long to pick up the news that Spanish golfing legend, Seve Ballesteros, had undergone a major operation to remove a brain tumour after collapsing on 6 October, just ten days ago.

There are a lot of hard and fast rules in The Hospital, yet they don't worry about people using cell phones, and they don't ask you what you are bringing into the Intensive Care Unit in the way of food. Craig's medical chart stated that he'd been eating too many sweets, so we decided not to take him more, although I did bake him a cake, which he and some of his ward mates relished. I told him we'd bring him apples and carrots next time!

I saw many doctors wandering about yesterday, so they're obviously back from Cape Town, and now we wait to see what they'll do next.

This is a huge struggle, but I've tried to keep my sense of humour, to save my sanity. Ian's way of dealing with this is quite different from mine. He doesn't talk about it, and tries not to be emotional, whereas I have to let it all out. We're attempting to take one step at a time, even when we feel that there are many rungs missing from this staircase.

Brian and Nicky are leaving tomorrow. May the Lord be with my littlest boy all the way as he pedals for his brother.

19 October 2008—Email

I plan to go back to work tomorrow. Amazing things are taking place. For example, Brian's holiday booking was cancelled due to a communication error. He and Nicky were very upset, because he was going to Durban not just to ride in the bicycle race for his brother; they were also looking forward to a week's break before his back surgery. They were told they wouldn't get a refund for the cancelled booking unless they could produce a doctor's letter saying that their brother was seriously ill. One would have to visit The Hospital to know that no one gets favours, and it's nigh on impossible to speak to a doctor even if close family are ill; so there seemed no way they could get a letter. We hadn't even had any updates on Craig's illness, and were in the dark about many things. On Friday we were all there when someone tapped Ian on the shoulder. He turned around to see a big, black Ghanaian fellow, a neurosurgeon, who happens to be interested in flying model aeroplanes, and who has been to the airfield a few times to get advice from Ian. (Ian is an aero modelling pilot and South African model aerobatics judge). This doctor gave us a thorough update on Craig's condition, supplied the letter for Brian and Nicky, and indulged us in some normal conversation. Things like that simply do not occur in that hospital! Thanks to Doug, Brian and Nicky found some alternative accommodation. They motored down to Durban, and Brian completed the race this morning. He says his back is fine, and we are thrilled by his achievement. They are now enjoying their little holiday.

Craig was much the same today, but so positive about his status that it flabbergasted me. He's determined to beat this thing, whatever it is. The doctors are speculating that it may not be what they originally thought, but we continue to wait for positive identification. Craig says the doctors told him this morning that he will have the MRI tomorrow. I hope so; this waiting is nerve-racking.

I've had a few hiccups about the hospital, but Craig is able to overlook all the things I that would call aggravations. Here's a for instance. There's a bathroom within the neurosurgical ward, but the bath is old and rusty and looks pretty dirty. There is no plug. I could never see myself getting into that bath. Craig, along with his drip stand, is able to walk to the bathroom. He says that he can't see the dirt, so will attempt a bath. He insists that he has bigger worries than the state of the bath—and so he has. It is apparent that the nursing staff respect his general attitude and they have bestowed upon him the name of Gentleman Craig. Not many patients get preferential treatment, but one nurse daily places a tub in the bath, fills it with water, and notifies him when his bath is ready! The walls need painting and the cockroaches are rife, but Gentleman Craig accepts it all, expecting no favours from anyone. All he wants is to get well.

Ian and I are bearing up. I cannot pretend it's easy, but I still have more strength than I would have thought possible. I have now counted six countries where people are praying for our son, thanks to my many friends around the world—Israel, America, Australia, Zimbabwe, South Africa, and England. I find this so encouraging.

Tuesday, 21 October 2008

There's still no word on when the MRI will be done, although Craig has been told that the time is drawing closer—an interesting piece of non-information indeed! Meanwhile he's confident that he will beat this thing. He's full of praise for the nursing staff, and he believes that God will heal him.

Craig can recognise people, but cannot read at all. His headaches are much less severe. He's been taken off some of the medication and has been permitted to walk around a bit. Constantly inspiring the people around him, he even jokes about his condition. I asked him if he talked to the other patients in the ward and he said yes, but it was difficult because it's a neurosurgical ward and patients have setbacks that affect their communication.

As he described it: "That guy over there slurs his words, so we can't figure out what he's saying, although he obviously knows. Another guy is too sick to speak, another guy is too depressed, and another has some other problem. And as for me—the nurses tell me that the other patients are waving at me, but I can't see them, so they think I'm being rude. What a bunch we are!"

One poor fellow has a tumour that causes him to have angry moments, which is very sad. One feels so helpless, trying to reach out to them, not knowing what to say. I'm able to speak a little Zulu, which helps, if only to greet them. People appreciate being spoken to in their own tongue, but I wish I could do more than that. I've never been amongst people with neurological disorders before, and although Craig is taking it all in his stride, it pains my heart. He's well aware that he's one of them; and so, regrettably, am I.

There was an extensive blackout in the city and surrounds yesterday, and all traffic lights were out, so it took us two and a quarter hours to get home from the hospital. These things are surely sent to try us. I was so exhausted by the end of the day, I felt like bursting into tears. I'd been to work for the morning, so it was a long day, but the good thing that came out of it was that I slept well last night, for the first time in a week that seemed like a year.

Friday, 24 October 2008—Email

We've had a couple of testing days, but we made it through them. Some days are harder to handle than others, and sometimes our figurative focus becomes a little blurred—just as Craig's literally does. His sight has been getting worse. He can't see much now, yet his hopes are high, and his positive attitude never ceases to amaze all the family. He doesn't take any notice of the hospital challenges, and he actually enjoys the food, which isn't as good as I thought it was. He says so what if the toilets are not what he's accustomed to. All he cares about is regaining his sight and getting back to his job, which he loves. What a lot we are learning through this experience! It teaches one the true value of life. The human race grumbles about such unimportant matters: we moan about doctors; we moan about nurses; we even moan about hospitals that don't have television! My word! Craig is blessed with friends and family who love him, and by the looks of things, he has good doctors and nursing staff around him. This is all he talks about, along with how his goal is to get well, get back to work, and get fit, because he has neglected personal fitness for so long. So now he wants a bicycle, too. What a boy!

I got the opportunity today to take my two younger sons by the hand and say a little prayer for their operations, which might be scheduled for the same day next week. Ian and I may well be running back and forth between two hospitals.

Chapter 3

I was with Craig when they came to take him down for his MRI scan. Because it was visiting hours, they let me go with him. He was capable of walking, but they put him in a wheelchair, which I told him was so he couldn't sneak off to find a corner where he could smoke. He wasn't amused with me. Whenever we visit him, he makes us march him down to the fifth floor, where there's an outside smoking area, and no amount of nagging is about to persuade him that this is a good time to quit. He says smoking de-stresses him, even though he is prepared to admit that it may have been what caused his problem in the first place. That debate will never end. One day Ian was his only visitor, so he was compelled to admit his addiction to his father when he asked him to escort him to the smoking area. So that hurdle in Craig's life has now been overcome.

The radiology section, in the lower part of the building, was spotless. Anxious people waited on plastic chairs, anticipating some unknown fate that was to surface from a great big metal machine, invented by a gentleman called Raymond Damadian; but they didn't know that, and I found out only through my inquisitive travels through the Internet. As we waited, we passed the time away with bits of idle chatter.

Out of the blue, Craig remarked, "D'you know that Seve had his second operation yesterday?"

"Who's Seve?" I asked

"Ballesteros, Mother, the world famous golfer from your era. I already told you he has a brain tumour."

"I know that. What do you mean, 'my era'?"

Craig grinned. He knew he'd get my attention with that remark.

I continued. "I'm still alive, Craigie boy. *This* is my era! Besides, he's at least ten years younger than I am."

"Oh no," he jested, "Your era has passed. This is *my* era. You're . . ."

I made sure I interrupted him. "Past my sell-by date? Now just you watch it, young man!"

"They say it's cancer," he said.

"Huh?"

"Seve. He's got cancer."

"Oh."

"Edwards, Craig," they called, and they came to take him away for the scan.

I sat reflecting on the events of the past two weeks. I thought of him going into that large cylindrical machine with its sliding bed that moves to and fro through the cylinder. I'd been in one of those claustrophobic gadgets, with that frightful hammering noise that beats upon your eardrums. They were supposed to give me earphones with music to dull the commotion, but that didn't happen, and I doubted they would do that in a state hospital. It was not a pleasant experience. Craig was probably having the dye injection, or contrast medium, to make the scan clearer. I chewed on my bit of chewed out gum. He'd deal with the scan, but would he deal with the results? Would I? It was cold in that section of the building. They had to keep the temperature down to cool the machine. I shivered. Next time, I'd bring a jacket, even in summer. MRI scanners use radio waves and magnets to provide an unparalleled view inside the human body without using surgery or X-rays. I'd have a lot of time in the future to read up on that.

Craig appeared with the radiographer about forty minutes later.

"How was it?" I asked.

"Well," he said, quite seriously, "Apart from the fact that I got whipped up by the magnetic force because of my metal braces . . ."

"Stop talking rubbish, Craig!"

The radiographer grinned. "This man is full of nonsense," she chortled, "When I asked him if he had any metal objects on him, he said, 'Only my magnetic personality!'"

"Tell my mom about the wheelchair," Craig said.

"I have to attend to the next patient," she responded, "You tell her."

The porter came to push Craig back to the ward, and on the way he related the wheelchair incident. A patient had been wheeled in to have an MRI scan. They keep the scanner running 24/7 because it apparently draws a huge amount of power each time it is switched off and on, and rebooting is a very expensive exercise. After the patient was helped out of the wheelchair, the magnetic energy of the machine lifted the chair into the air and threw it against the scanner with incredible force. No number of people were able to pull it off. The scanner had to be switched off and was found to be damaged by the impact. Repairs and reconnection ran into the thousands, and a few people found themselves in a spot of trouble.

"I wonder what would have happened," Craig mused, "if the patient had still been in the wheelchair on impact. Splat!"

Craig's wittiness triumphed over my deep-seated fear of the unfamiliar path ahead.

We've come to know some of the other patients and their families, some of whom have been there for months; but others, like Craig, are newcomers. I think that many of them have little or no support, and when I see all the encouraging emails we are getting, it hardly seems fair. They probably don't even have computers, let alone friends around the world.

One day when I was visiting a strange man walked into the ward carrying a small paper bag.

"Hello Craig," he said, "How are you doing?"

Craig strained his eyes to make out the image in front of him, but seemed to recognise the voice. "Mr Robinson?"

Mr Robinson smiled. "That's me. I brought you this." He handed the bag to Craig, who was bowled over by this man's visit.

"That's so kind of you," he said. "How did you know I was here?"

"The man in your shop told me, so I thought I'd pop in, but I'll leave you with your family now."

"Thank you," Craig stammered, "Thank you."

Mr Robinson made a hurried getaway as Craig opened the bag. Inside was a box of chocolates and a small book of the Gospel of St. John.

I aimed to run after Mr Robinson, but he'd already taken the elevator.

"I don't believe it," Craig was saying. "He's one of my customers. He used to come into the shop, and if I had a headache, he would pray for me."

I stood there with my mouth open, thinking it was a shame there weren't more Mr Robinsons in the world. Craig was paging through the book.

"Can you read that print, Craig?" I asked.

"No, but I will when I've had my operation," he replied.

The next day he told me that one of the neurosurgeons had picked up the book and asked him where it came from. He said he'd appreciate one of those. I was so moved by all of this that I went to a Christian bookshop and bought another copy, which I told Craig to give to the doctor the next time he called. Craig was such a character! On my next visit, I noticed that the book was gone, so I asked him if he'd given it to the doctor.

"I don't know," he answered. "They all look the same to me because I can't see properly."

"What do you mean?"

"Well, some black doctor came in here and I gave it to him. I don't know if it was the same one."

"But he took it anyway?" I spouted.

"Yup. There must be something captivating about that book."

I sniggered. The following week I made some enquiries and located Mr Robinson. I told him I'd keep him posted.

"You've got a fine son there," he said.

"I know."

Reports on Seve Ballesteros say that his tumour has been removed. Craig is still awaiting his first operation, with no indication as to when it will take place. That's one difference between private and state hospitals. It will be interesting to see if the final outcome is any different. I don't suppose Craig ever thought he'd have anything in common with a world famous golfer. Life is acutely unpredictable.

Wednesday, 29 October 2008—Email

Yesterday was a stressful day, but it's gone and we handled it. There are days when I feel so tired and drained that I can barely stand up, and yet I know with every fibre of my being that God is in control.

Brian's surgery went well. He has two metal replacement discs at the top of his spine and all he has to show for it is a small cut on one side of the front of his neck. He was looking remarkably healthy and joking soon after he came out of the theatre. He's in a good hospital and expects to be out in a couple of days.

I was on the way to see him in the afternoon, intending to visit with Craig after that, when I received a call from Craig to say he'd received the results of the MRI scan.

"A massive tumour," was all he could say.

We already knew that from the CAT scan, but Craig was told that the MRI would be used to identify the intricacies of the tumour for the purpose of the biopsy, which is apparently scheduled for next week. In the meantime, the doctors told him to go home and wait to be called in for surgery. They said he'll have to wait at least a week after the surgery for the results. A surgeon informed him that if they can remove it, or part of it, it will probably have to be done in a series of operations. Otherwise they'll try to shrink it, or whatever. I'm beginning to get the impression that some of these doctors will say anything to humour the patients. There's so much uncertainty about when things will happen, or even whether they will happen at all, so they tell people what they think they want to hear, and the next day another doctor tells them a completely different story. I'm starting to think that seeing is believing at The Hospital.

Despite the demands of yesterday, I still look forward to all our tomorrows. Speaking of tomorrow, it's Craig's thirty-seventh birthday, so we're having the family for dinner, and I'm sure we'll all enjoy it. My birthday is the next day, so we often celebrate our birthdays jointly.

How is Craig feeling? Remarkably strong and positive, so much so that when I phoned him last night, he was the one who made me feel better. I've never let him know if I'm a bit down, so ever a brave face; but I was feeling down, and he was saying such optimistic things that I felt rather ashamed of myself. He says he knows the seriousness of this tumour, but that if the doctors tell him there's nothing they can do, he's got news for them! He says he has more than enough faith to believe that he will be healed, doctors or no doctors! He's pleased to be at home, because two weeks was long enough for him in that establishment. He was getting fed up with being idle. Better to do nothing at home, he says. He tries to watch TV, but mostly just follows the sound. This morning he said the only thing he tripped over was the vacuum cleaner, but that didn't matter because he has a lump in his head anyway! To be able to laugh under these circumstances is such a godsend.

Chapter 4

I found it hard to believe that a patient could be sent home in Craig's condition, but we were to discover that there would be many things that would be difficult to fathom in the months to come. It's common knowledge in South Africa that there are all kinds of untoward happenings in state hospitals, although I've heard that this particular hospital is one of the best. We were to contend with endless irritations. Staff shortages, long queues, run-down sanitation, and the extreme frustration caused by incompetent administration were just a few of them; but I quickly realised that when someone's life is at stake, such problems don't seem quite as important as they may otherwise have been. That said, they do increase one's stress levels and tend to make one dreadfully worn out by the end of what feels like a forty-eight hour day. Irritations, however, are one thing. Total botch-ups are another.

Nevertheless, I have much good to say about many of the people we encountered over the years in The Hospital. I've seen doctors practically pulling their hair out due to incompetency and the shortages with which they have to deal, yet I've been humbled by much of what I've seen in the wards, clinics, and corridors of that hospital. I've seen patients helping and encouraging one another; and non-complaining, sick people waiting in very long queues to see doctors, or get medicine. In the neuro clinic, I've seen mothers tending to babies with grossly enlarged heads, which I was told are commonly due to enlarged brains, or cerebral fluid on the brain, causing blindness, convulsions and mental disability. These mothers know that their children will probably live only a few years, and yet they sit in waiting rooms for hours, desperately holding on to every last bit of hope.

When Craig was originally diagnosed, we knew little to nothing at all about brain tumours. We were to learn a lot. Often we were misinformed by staff members, sometimes even by doctors. There are many interns in training hospitals, and their inexperience can lead to wrong interpretation of reports or incorrect assumptions when they can't find a report. This happened to us a few times.

Of the family, it was more convenient for me to do most of the ferrying to and from the hospital, because I had a flexible part-time job. We usually had to travel during peak hours, and it took at least an hour to get there from Benoni. I spent more time there with Craig than anyone else, and thus became familiar with the ins and outs of hospital protocol. Many times he didn't absorb what the doctors were telling him, so he'd give twisted versions of their findings. Thankfully, he was willing, in fact eager, for me to accompany him into the consulting rooms, because I'd get a first-hand report of every assessment. He'd repeatedly ask me what the doctors had said, and then he'd go home and tell the family something that didn't quite match up to what had actually been said. One thing that never changed was his positivity, ever assuring people he was going to be fine, and meaning it. I never once heard him complain, or ask, "Why me?" even after he was given the worst conceivable prognosis.

The Hospital has well over a thousand beds and a staff of over four thousand. It is the main teaching hospital for a major South African university. Being an academic institution, all patients need to be referred, and only priority one and two emergency patients, whose lives are in danger, will be seen without a referral. Even so, a major shortage of beds is the order of the day. There's a long waiting list for X-rays and other treatment, and another long waiting list for operating theatres. People die waiting for beds. Some get beds and then die in them while waiting for a slot in the operating theatre. Some patients occupy beds for weeks on end, in the hopes that they will soon find a space in the theatre and a surgeon who is available to operate. And while patients occupy beds, waiting for surgery, others die at home, waiting for beds.

There's no such thing as a proper appointment in a South African state hospital. You are told to come on Friday. If you are sensible, you get there early. Invariably you wait a few hours to see a doctor. Then you wait a few more hours in the pharmacy to get your medication, perhaps another hour or two to get a blood test, and so on. Everything takes hours, so you get up at 5:00 a.m. and write off the rest of your day. That's how it works.

As I wrote the initial diary of events relating to Craig's progress, I was frequently under some sort of delusion, whereby I was led to assume that prearranged events would actually come about within the specified time slot. I eventually accepted the truth. African time is not the same as time elsewhere in the world! This becomes evident in the following pages.

Saturday, 1 November 2008—Email

Thanks for all the mails, text messages, and phone calls, and a big thank you to my friend Linda for a really gorgeous meal that she brought over the other day. Nicky shared some of it with us when Brian was in hospital, and we have some left for this weekend. We don't expect all this special treatment, but thank you anyway! Thanks also for all the birthday wishes for Craig and me. My birthday was quiet and relaxing—the first day in three weeks that we have not had to go to one hospital or another.

We had a lovely birthday dinner on Thursday night, and it will remain special for me forever. It's true that when the going gets tough, the tough get going! This is tough for Craig, but he is truly a hero. Brian bought him an original Liverpool football shirt for his birthday and he was delighted with that—he's a Liverpool fanatic!

At his home on his 37th birthday

Brian's doing well, albeit a bit disappointed because he still can't lift his right arm, although he thinks it may be a little better, but needs to give it time. His doctors didn't know if he would regain the full use of his arm by having this op, but they hoped so. At any rate, he needed to have the two discs replaced, because he was in a lot of pain. His neck's a bit stiff, but he's looking well and is confident that his arm will recover.

We'll all be spending special time with Craig this weekend before he goes back into hospital on Monday. Optimistically, he won't have to wait more than a day or two for his surgery.

Wednesday, 5 November 2008—Email

Craig was told to check in on Monday the second, but after waiting for two hours, he was sent home because there was no bed for him. He kept phoning on Tuesday and today (Wednesday), but has been told that there's no chance of being admitted this week. It appears that a number of seriously ill patients were transferred there from another hospital. They're saying that as long as he's managing on the medication they've given him, he's not at the top of the list. This is exceedingly stressful for all of us, but we can't do anything about it. It's frightening to know that our son has a huge, aggressive tumour, which is seriously affecting his eyesight, and right now no one is doing anything about it. He's been told to report to the neurosurgical clinic early on Friday morning, because his medication will be finished by then, and he'll need a new prescription. We hope a doctor will be able to give him some indication of what they plan to do, but of course, we already know that what they plan to do is not likely to be what they actually do.

I am reminded of what Abraham Lincoln said: "I have been many times driven to my knees by the overwhelming conviction that I had nowhere else to go." How true! I'm certainly on my knees now.

Friday, 7 November 2008—Email

We've just crossed another hurdle; Craig is back in hospital. Georgie took him there before 8:00 a.m. this morning to get his medication, but he had taken his bag in the hope of being admitted. After a few hours of waiting, they admitted him at 1:30 p.m. With a bit of luck, this means that he'll have the surgery early next week. He's relieved to be there because he now has a foot in the door so to speak. This has taken a load off our minds, and even though we don't know what's in store, at least there are prospects of getting this surgery done soon. Ian and I will be running around between work and the hospital again next week.

Monday, 10 November 2008

Surgery is scheduled for tomorrow morning. Craig saw the anaesthetist this evening and says she's a congenial woman who gave him confidence. We should be able to see him in the afternoon. He has no idea which doctor from the team of neurosurgeons will operate.

We've waited a month to get to this point, and what a month it has been. Considering that Craig almost lost his life the night he was admitted to hospital, this is outrageous but unhappily, it's customary in South Africa if one doesn't have medical aid. To say that people die waiting is no exaggeration. I recently heard of a case of one such person who also had a brain tumour. By the grace of God, our son is still alive, but I would be untruthful if I said that I wasn't afraid. My greatest fear in life has been that I might lose one of my children. I'm scared. I'm very, very scared.

Chapter 5

The waiting seemed endless. Sitting in my sun lounge, I watched dozens of doves swooping down to eat the birdseed that Ian had thrown down early that morning. The big glass windows in that room lend themselves to bird watching, but I wasn't thinking about birds, even though I was watching them. I tried to picture the operating theatre, with students lined up, ready to observe the neurosurgeon cutting into my son's scalp and the piece of skull over the tumour. The flap would then be flipped, giving access to the tumour. That's what I'd heard. Blood would be available, in case of excess bleeding, which I'd been told was common with brain surgery. I didn't want to think about it, but I couldn't help it. Who was this doctor? Was he experienced, or was he one of the interns, performing his first brain operation? It was a training hospital, after all. So was he a learner, or a trainer? I consoled myself with the thought that if he was a learner, then a qualified surgeon would need to be standing over him, or her. But I didn't want that. I wanted only the best for my son. This, however, was a government institution, and one couldn't demand the best. I hated the not knowing part. No one even knew what time they would operate, so I kept phoning to see if he was still in the ward. When his phone went on to voicemail, I knew he'd gone to theatre—the eleventh hour of the eleventh day of the eleventh month. My body froze. I felt so alone. I sensed that my son was so alone. I hadn't been able to pray that morning, but

I was sitting with my Bible on my lap. Something in my spirit prompted me to randomly open it and my eyes fell upon these words from Isaiah 48, verse 16 (NIV):

> Come near me and listen to this: From the first announcement I have not spoken in secret; at the time it happens, I am there.

God had spoken to me, and I was instantly overcome by a deep sense of peace. With tears pouring down my cheeks, the neurosurgeon in my mind became the best. I knew that he was competent, and I knew that he would do his utmost to save my son's life and enable him to live a normal life. We were later to find out that he was the top neurosurgeon in the hospital, the head of the department of neurosurgery.

Ian, Georgie, and I arrived at the hospital at exactly 3:00 p.m. Surgery was still in progress, so we waited in the passageway outside the neurosurgical ward. It was a long, wide passage, which lead to the theatre, and the wait was long too. With only two plastic chairs between the three of us, Ian did the gentlemanly thing and stood the whole time. His job requires him to be on his feet all day, so this added to the sore feet he already had. 5:00 p.m. came and the security guards didn't kick us out. As odd as that may sound, that is what they do. They walk around with batons, which I would hope are purely for the sake of appearances. It was 6:00 p.m. when we saw two women wheeling Craig down the passage. We ran to meet him. He was hooked up to a drip, head bandaged, but he was smiling, saying hi to us. Then it happened. They turned the corner to take him into the ward, smashing the bed into the door, denting its metal rim. Three years later, I noted that the door was still dented. We couldn't believe our eyes!

Craig bolted upright in the bed, holding his head, with a loud, "Aah !"

Georgie was shouting, "You idiots! Don't you know he just had a brain operation?"

I was too stunned to say anything. Without uttering a word, the two women straightened the bed and continued their journey into the intensive care unit. We had to sit around for half an hour whilst they settled him in ICU, but when we eventually got in to see him at 6.30 p.m., he was looking exceptionally well. He was fully alert and even though he was wired up to many tubes and breathing apparatus, he couldn't stop talking about how good it was that he'd been in there for such a long time because they must have removed at least some of the tumour! I would jolly well hope so! We had only a few minutes with him, but the relief was indescribable. We'll be seeing him this afternoon, and we expect to be told what they found. Praise the Lord that he can see, though we don't know how well.

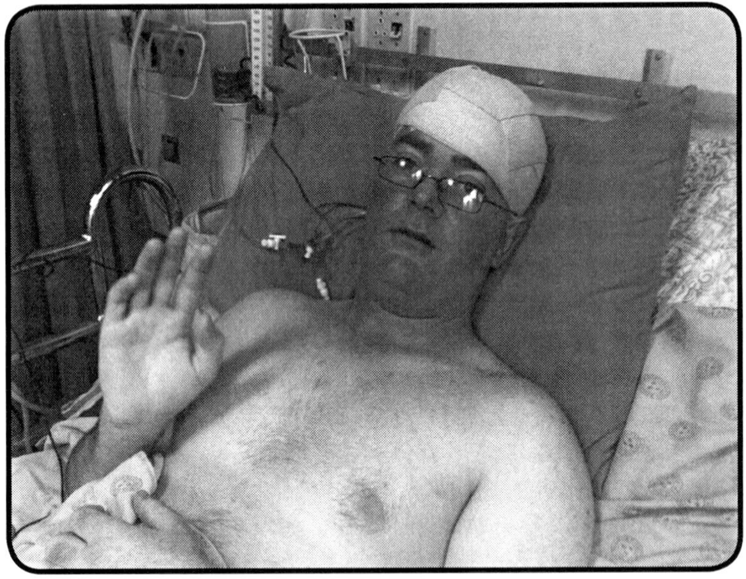

The day after his first operation

Wednesday, 12 November 2008—Email

Craig is out of ICU already and now in the high care unit and full of nonsense! Since this hospital doesn't supply pillows—at least that section doesn't—he had given strict instructions to ensure we collected his personal pillow from the ward he'd been in before the op. The nursing staff had kept his pillow and his glasses. When he came out of theatre, he wasn't allowed to have a pillow, and Georgie decided that she would collect his belongings from the other ward the next day. Well—did *that* turn out to be a bad move! When we finally got to see him again, at visiting hours the following day, he was furious about not having his pillow because his head was sorely uncomfortable. He complained that he couldn't see because he didn't have his glasses and so couldn't tell if his sight had been affected by the surgery. He was inconsolably grumpy. Adding to his discomfort was a tube going into his head to drain excess blood from the wound. When he did get his glasses, he was disappointed, because he couldn't detect any change to his eyesight. We tried to tell him it was early days and perhaps he'd see more clearly once the swelling subsided. The fact is, we don't know. It would help to know a bit more about brain surgery. It would help to be able to see one of his doctors. It would help to be patient. I think we're going to need patience; after all, it's been a whole month since Craig was rushed to hospital with a seizure on that near-fatal night.

Today was another very tiring day. After driving miles to the hospital, we walked up many flights of stairs to visit Craig, because the elevators weren't working. The size of that outfit never ceases to amaze me. *It's huge!*

Yesterday, whilst we were waiting hours for him to come out of surgery, someone was talking about Mr Bean, and I decided that he should come to South Africa and make a movie in The Hospital. It would make millions and would be the best Mr Bean move ever made! That place is geared up for that fellow! A little amusement is food for the soul. There are many obstacles, but we'll have to make the best of this, because it could be a long haul.

The doctor who operated told Craig this morning that the samples have gone off to the pathology lab for analysis and that they removed as much of the tumour as they could; but it was widespread, and trying to remove it all would have been dangerous. He wasn't able to say when the biopsy results would be available. Our motto will have to be "Patience, learn patience". Craig is still uncomfortable, but if all continues to go well, they will soon take the tube out of his head and remove the bandages. He's no longer on a drip, and they've stopped the medication that he was on before the operation. It sounds as though all he's having is some form of anti-inflammatory and paracetemol for the headaches.

Ian will be visiting Craig tomorrow, but I've decided to give it a miss because I'll be working in the morning, and running my Weigh-Less group in the late afternoon. I've had to get other ladies to stand in for me lately, because the visiting hours clash with my classes, but I have to try and get back to some form of routine.

Sunday, 16 November 2008

To our amazement, Craig was discharged yesterday (Saturday). He had the op on Tuesday, and was remarkably well on Wednesday and Thursday; but on Friday he was in a lot of discomfort and generally feeling down, which is to be expected after major surgery. He seemed to think it was because they had doubled his medication, which made him feel under the weather, so it wasn't a good day. Imagine my surprise when I heard that he was going home on Saturday. All things considered, he had quite a good night on Friday, and in the morning he asked the doctor to discharge him. The place was getting him down, and he felt he'd be much better off in the comfort of his own home. The ward is overcrowded once again, and some of the patients are so ill that it's depressing to be amongst them. Craig has boxes of medication and has to rest a lot, but when I phoned him this morning, he was watching movies and seemed to be fine. He says there's minimal improvement to his vision, but I think he's managing to read the subtitles on the TV. Ian and I went to see him at home yesterday afternoon; compared to the day before, he was looking great. He has no bandages or dressings on the wound, but was wearing a bandana, which I'm sure he never thought he'd be doing! I've been told that cuts the size of his are the norm for brain ops, but Ian and I were stunned when we saw it. He has thirty-five clips in his head, and the semicircular wound measures twelve inches. No wonder it's uncomfortable to lie on.

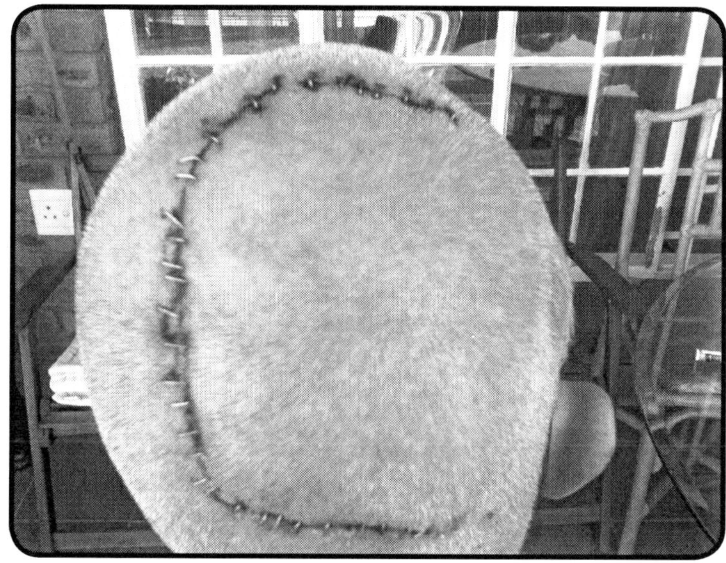

At home with 35 clips in his head

He's due to go to Outpatients to have the clips out on Friday and will not see a neurosurgeon unless there are complications. The staff have said they'll contact him once they have the histology report, which they are now saying takes about two weeks from the time of the operation, so patience is still the name of the game. We have no idea what the procedure will be after that. The back of his head is quite swollen on the one side, and we are hoping that once that goes down the pressure will be relieved and he will regain his sight.

Brian, in the meantime, has managed to lift his arm a little higher than he could before his operation, with the help of anti-inflammatories. He was X-rayed last week, and the replacement discs are neatly in place.

Sunday, 23 November 2008

Craig has been battling with pain and, I suppose, boredom, but he has plenty of medication. I haven't had a good week, but am determined that it will get better. One thing I've learned recently is that when you're faced with an unexpected situation, you simply have to deal with it. If you don't, you'll end up in an even worse place. You don't think that anything like this could happen to you; in fact, you don't think about it at all. Then boom! Your priorities change overnight. The things you worried about yesterday seem vaguely insignificant. The problems are still there, but they're suddenly easier to overcome than you ever thought they could be.

Friday, 28 November 2008—Email

We don't have the biopsy results yet. I feel sure they're ready, but although Craig has been told to phone the head neurosurgeon to get them, he's simply never available. The sad thing with government organisations in this country is that you cannot rely on people who say they will call you back, and you don't even know if the person you are trying to contact received your message. And so it goes. Craig is due to see a neurosurgeon at the clinic on 12 December, and it could turn out that he won't know the results before then. We're getting the hang of the way things work in The Hospital now. The idea is to go early in the morning and wait as long as it takes to see a doctor, which we have learned is invariably hours. Last week there were 250 people waiting in the pharmacy for medication. Fortunately, when they realised that Craig was blind, they put him in the disabled queue, and he didn't have to wait too long.

It's been difficult for me to talk about this blindness up to now, because I can't accept that the damage to his eyes is permanent, and I still believe with all my heart that it will improve. Today I had a chat with Craig; I told him that I believe no matter what happens, good will come out of this. If his eyesight doesn't improve, then I know that God has other plans for him. He may have to totally change his way of life, but there is light at the end of this dark tunnel, be it literal light or not.

He says he can't describe his vision, except to say that what he sees is not what we see, but a peculiar type of vision, which doesn't last long. Some mornings he wakes up totally blind. Then, after some minutes of adjustment, he can make out shapes and sees just a little. Occasionally he can read a message on a cell phone, but only by looking at it, looking away, and trying to adjust to the letters; so it takes quite a long time. Sometimes he watches a bit of TV, until the picture disappears; then he gets frustrated and can't be bothered with it. He says it's difficult to concentrate on anything, because of the continual adjusting he has to do. Whatever the results of the biopsy, a neurosurgeon has told him that his vision is beyond repair, because both optic nerves are permanently damaged. Therefore, Craig has been declared disabled. However, I for one will not give up hope. The waiting is still the hardest part. I refuse to doubt that Craig will be able to work again. He doesn't doubt that either, although he may have to make some adjustments, and he's willing to do that. The good news is that the headaches aren't nearly so bad now, and he has stopped taking the painkillers, which were so strong that it frightened all of us. He's taking Epilim (to stop seizures), but has cut down that dosage quite drastically since the operation. I don't think he's supposed to do that, but Craig will be Craig, and no one can convince him to take pills when he's not feeling ill. The wound is healing well, and his hair is growing again, so he's looking better.

I'm so grateful to God for all He has done for our family. Knowing that our son is in His hands is the most comforting thought, even when the days are a bit gloomy.

Saturday, 6 December 2008

Someone told Craig that the biopsy results are available, but the neurosurgeons aren't prepared to discuss them over the phone, so he'll get them on Friday the twelfth, when he goes for his check-up. A few days ago he gained full vision for a couple of hours, except for a blind spot on one side. It seems when he moves around, his vision comes and goes, which although rather weird, does tie in with the original diagnosis of oedema of his optic nerves. At present his eyesight is extremely poor. He cannot drive, read, or do anything of value with this type of vision.

Whoever invented the term *waiting game* was obviously inexperienced in it, or just stupid! This is definitely not a game! Friday, 12 December will be exactly two months since that frightening seizure, so to see him walking, talking, eating, and even telling jokes about people with brain tumours is surely a blessing. I'm not partial to the jokes he tells, but the principle is good. Yesterday he told us that if a nuclear bomb went off, he'd be the only one who wasn't negatively affected because the radiation would probably sort out his brain tumour. *Not funny!*

Chapter 6

There's no other way to say this—The Hospital has lost the biopsy results.

Friday, 12 December 2008, was the longest day ever. I left home at 6:00 a.m. to collect Craig, who lives about fifteen kilometres away. I dropped him off at home over twelve hours later. We arrived at the hospital at 7:15 a.m. There were three surgeons on duty in the neurosurgical clinic and hundreds of patients waiting to see them, but the queue was moving quickly, and we waited only two and a half hours before gaining access to a consulting room.

It was my first encounter with the Indian doctor I would come to know and respect. His opening remark was to greet us and ask Craig how he was feeling. He appeared a little vague as he looked through the uninformative file.

"What did the histology show?" he asked.

I smiled. "You tell us, Doctor."

"I'm asking you," the surgeon said, "because there's nothing in this file."

Craig, being Craig, never said a word.

I stared at the surgeon. "We've waited over a month for these results, Doctor. Are you saying they aren't in yet?"

Puzzled would not aptly describe the surgeon's face.

"There's no report here," he said, picking up the phone, "The lab must still have it."

But they didn't. Neither did the neuro ward. He checked every place where it might be, to no avail.

"Wait here," he said, "I'm going to get to the bottom of this."

About ten minutes later, he came back. "I don't know what to say," he said apologetically. "All reports are supposed to be on computer, but Craig's isn't, and this organisation has no backup system."

I was gobsmacked. "What?"

He was highly embarrassed. "I'm so, so sorry," he said, "This is shocking, but it's the truth. There is absolutely nothing I can do about it."

Craig, being the typically unfazed person that he is, said something to the effect that he supposed these things happen. The surgeon promised to phone if anything came to light, but of course we were all wondering exactly when the report disappeared. Probably weeks ago. I would also not be surprised if the specimen never even reached the pathology lab and there never was a report. After a massive operation, they lose the critical evidence! When I asked if this was a common occurrence, the surgeon said yes and proceeded to remind me that this was a government hospital and we live in South Africa. To that I had no reply, because it went without saying. Not only were we anxious to hear once and for all that there was no cancer, but the knowledge of what type of tumour this was would have determined what treatment the doctors would have to do.

"I'm banging my head against a brick wall," the surgeon said. "This sort of thing happens all the time."

I was stunned, as Craig slowly came to the realisation of the seriousness of this matter.

The doctor shook his head, once again examining the pictures of Craig's brain.

"Let's have another look at these scans," he said, "We have nothing else to go on."

Bearing in mind that these scans had been taken before the surgery, I was dubious about learning anything more than we already knew, which was practically nothing anyway. The doctor put both the CAT scan and the MRI on the screen, explaining what he felt the way forward should be. I'd never seen any of the scans, because I didn't want to. But I think that was the right time for me to see them, because the doctor put positive thoughts into our heads. He said there was quite a lot of calcification on the tumour, a good sign, because cancerous tumours rarely calcify, so he was hopeful that the tumour was benign. Because he did not perform the operation, he didn't know how much had been removed, but he suggested another CAT scan, which would show the current size of the tumour. In his opinion, the tumour needed to be removed, whether it was malignant or not. He felt that neither radiation therapy, nor chemotherapy was the answer, but the decision would be made after the next CAT scan. He added that he didn't consider this to be urgent or life-threatening. Therefore it didn't matter that we were now into the Christmas holiday season when many things come to a halt in government establishments.

"I want you to have a blood test," he said, "and then you can book appointments for a scan and another visit here in January. We'll take it from there."

He handed us a prescription for a month's medication, and we left with half a smile and a handshake. I couldn't help wondering how many more histology reports would be lost that day.

From there we had to find the blood section, where the queue for a blood test was a half hour long. Then off we went for a half-mile walk (I mean that) to the place where they do CAT scans, so we could book an appointment for the new year. There were all sorts of procedures and little stickers had to be stuck on everything, about which I could write a book! We booked the CAT scan for 13 January, then trudged back to the neuro clinic to stand in another queue to book the appointment to see a neurosurgeon on 23 January. Of course, it probably won't be the same neurosurgeon, and sadly, they don't necessarily agree, but the good news is that there is a plan—we think! Nothing is cast in stone in government hospitals. This is so frustrating and stressful.

By then it was noon and we both needed a little rest, so we dropped the prescription off in the pharmacy and went to the canteen where we had a Coke and a small packet of crisps each. Sitting there, we phoned the family to tell them about the lost biopsy results. Everyone was horrified.

At 12:30 p.m. we arrived back at the pharmacy to collect the medication, which the doctor had said Craig will probably have to take for the rest of his life. My word—we were number 745 in the queue! They start the numbering when they open at 8:00 a.m. daily, and at this stage they were up to number 420. There were only 324 patients in front of us! The waiting area was almost full, but we managed to find two seats together.

After two hours I was afraid to get up and go to the loo because I knew Craig wouldn't be able to hold my seat, and there was a long wait ahead. If people see a vacant seat in that pharmacy, they grab it. They're not interested in who needs to go to the loo. Of course, it stands to reason you don't want to go to the loo unless you're desperate. You have to be desperate to use those loos, especially the ones on the fifth floor, where the neuro clinic is. They are revolting. The doors don't have handles, let alone latches, two of the three loos don't have seats (not that I'd sit on them if they did) and there is never any toilet paper, or towels on which to dry your hands. There is no soap to wash your hands, and once there wasn't even any water in the taps. Often, people don't flush the toilets, but I think I've said enough. After three hours, I was desperate, so I plucked up the courage to go. I walked into the ladies room and held my breath until I got out. On my return to the pharmacy, my seat was still vacant because the crowd was dwindling and there was no one standing.

After four and a half hours, Craig's number was called and we took possession of the medication. We left the hospital at 5:00 p.m., in time for the peak hour traffic. To crown it all, I drove home in a torrential storm, and none of the traffic lights were working. Craig was doing some serious back-seat driving, and I told him to shut up because he was blind and couldn't see what was going on anyway! Appalling mother? Not really. One has to make light of things periodically. He does it himself. Laughter is good medicine.

Thus it was over twelve hours from the time we left to the time we returned. I dropped Craig at his house and drove home, thoroughly exhausted. It was to become the norm after visiting the hospital that the first thing I'd do when I got home would be to run the bath water, then disappear beneath it, head and all.

Despite the irritations, there is a lighter side. I always take my crocheting with me when I know we'll be waiting for hours. The seating in the pharmacy comprises metal chairs joined together in rows. Each time I commence crocheting, Craig complains that I'm rocking the boat.

"Well, sonny, you'll have to put up with it," I say, "Because I ain't sitting here all day doing nothing!" So the crochet movement continues, the blanket grows, and sonny boy is obliged to go along for the ride!

Sunday, 14 December 2008

Has this been a further test of my faith. Oh yes—in fact this morning I had a good deal to say to God about it. As my beautiful French Congolese friend, Wivine, would say, "God is on the control." What a devoted prayer companion she has been. I'm sure she's had the whole Congolese community praying for our son. I wish I could mention everyone who's praying for him, but they know who they are, and I thank them all. God listens, and He will answer in His way, in His time.

Once again, we face tomorrow with an element of trepidation. Craig has an extraordinary capability of being able to take one day at a time without letting his thoughts jump ahead of him. There's so much to consider, not the least of which is finance and what he'll be able to do for a living with his limited vision, unable to drive a car.

Chapter 7

Christmas 2008 was a family occasion that will always hold precious memories. We celebrated at our home, with gifts around the Christmas tree and the traditional ham and turkey dinner. But the best part was that Craig was with us. We didn't know what lay ahead, but I think it's a good thing we can't see into the future, because that knowledge would be hard to bear. I believe we should do our best to live for today because worrying about the future is not going to change anything that tomorrow may bring. As we stepped into 2009 my hopes for our son were as high as they'd ever been. I'd be lying if I said I had no fears, but I managed to allay them by focusing on my trust in the Lord.

Saturday, 17 January 2009—Email

Having had his CAT scan on Tuesday, Craig will be seeing a neurosurgeon next week. I do hope they don't lose the scans. He was forced to leave his previous CAT scan and MRI with the radiologist because they need them to do a comparison between before and after the surgery, so if they lose them, then all evidence of everything that has happened to him will have gone down the chute. Oh, that's not entirely true—he will still have a massive scar underneath his hair to prove that he had surgery! I know I shouldn't joke about this, but I was very dubious about leaving those scans at The Hospital. Craig told the radiographer the story about the lost biopsy results, and she assured him he would get all the scans back, including the latest one. I still don't think that specimen ever reached the laboratory. Who knows?

Tuesday was the best day we've had at that hospital. A long queue for the scanner welcomed us, but somehow Craig and two others were chosen to go to another department, where the wait was short, and we were out of there in just over two hours, a record time indeed. We have to collect the scans immediately before we get into the queue to see the surgeon on Friday. The radiographer seemed positive, and so am I. Meanwhile Craig is holding his own. He has a bad reaction to bright lights and says that travelling by car at night, with oncoming vehicle lights coming towards him, is painful to his eyes. He tends to get upset if anyone takes a photo of him with a flashlight. Although his headaches are frequent, they are not severe. People have been amazed by his optimism. He never grumbles and hardly speaks about his condition.

Sunday, 24 January 2009—Email

A sincere thank you for your prayers, and those of some of your friends around the world whom we don't even know, and for the interest you've shown in our son over the past few months. Many of you have not met him, yet you have passed my emails on to others and because of that we've received a number of letters from individuals we'd never heard of until our son became ill. I'm quite sure that many of you have troubles of your own, yet have found the time to add our son to your prayer list. God bless you, and may He hold you up in your own times of need.

I took Craig to see a neurosurgeon yesterday, after the CAT scan that was done a couple of weeks ago. It shows that most of the tumour has been removed. There's still a small portion left, and they may decide to remove that at a later date, but the surgeon feels that this is a slow-growing tumour. Half a dozen neurosurgeons have agreed that a malignant tumour would have spread rapidly, so this one is therefore being regarded as benign. The surgeon that we saw yesterday said that any brain tumour, whether malignant or benign, is dangerous. His words were that "anything inside a person's head which is not the way God designed it to be should not be there, no matter what it is". However, he said because tampering with the brain is risky, and there is presently no threat, it would be best to leave what's left of the tumour for the next three months and then reassess the situation, probably with another MRI scan, which gives more detail than the CAT scan. He didn't exactly say so, but my feeling was that it would be a bit too traumatic to operate again now. So let's wait and see what this tumour does over a period of a few months. In the meantime, Craig will continue on the medication to lessen the likelihood of seizures.

When asked about his vision, the surgeon confirmed what the other doctor had said: the residual visual deficit is due to his optic nerves being damaged, and this is irreversible. I still look forward to the day when he can drive a car again, which I believe will come. Meanwhile, he can read, write, watch television, and work (or play!) on the computer. He has a much bigger blind spot than everyone else, and because he can't see them, he bumps into people who walk on the left side of him. He says he can't see people who are shorter than he is unless he moves his head downwards, because he can't see other than straight ahead merely by moving his eyes. He explains that when most people walk, they look ahead, not downwards, but they are able to move their eyes up and down and thus see objects that are shorter or taller than them. Craig has to move his whole head down in order to see anything below eye-level, so if he's walking along, focussing on what is ahead of him, he is likely to bump into anyone who is shorter than he is! He finds the whole scenario difficult to explain. I suppose he thinks it sounds odd to say he can't see you if you are shorter than he is; after all, he's six feet two inches tall, which must mean he can't see most people!

Yesterday wasn't too much of an ordeal. I was away from home for only nine hours, as contrasted with twelve the last time we saw a doctor. It's mainly the waiting for the medicine that's so tiresome, but we'll have to get used to that, as his medicine has to be collected once a month, and the wait last time was five hours. Yesterday was only three, but we've gotten smart now. We drop off the prescription, go and sit in the canteen for an hour, then go back to wait till Craig's number is called out. Once you have a seat in the pharmacy, you keep it. You have to be there when your number comes up, otherwise—well who knows—maybe they lose the medicine, as they lost the biopsy report! We can see the funny side now, but some things that occur in that hospital are quite scary. I found someone else's CAT scans in Craig's envelope recently. They were dated April 2008, so I do wonder what transpired there. I took them back to the radiology department yesterday, and the reaction was "Oh dear." Said scans were then placed on top of a pile of documents and probably sent to File 13. I know it was none of my business, but I asked what would be done about that poor patient's missing scans that had now come to light.

"Oh, I don't know," was the casual reply, "They're months old, and we've probably lost track of the patient by now. He might even be dead."

Doesn't this speak volumes?

Sunday, 25 January 2009

Now Craig can start making decisions about what he will do for a living under the circumstances of not being able to drive, along with a few other limitations. Thank God he can see, because not long ago he was almost completely blind from time to time. He would have unexpected blackouts for minutes at a time, when he was unable to see at all. Before the operation, he was feeling his way to the bathroom. And one time when we encountered him in the elevator, he didn't see us at all. What was he doing alone in the elevator? He had left the ward, with permission from the senior nurse, to wander down to the smoking area on the fifth floor. He keeps insisting that cigarettes help to suppress his headaches, which to me, is ridiculous, but I suppose it is conceivable that the so-called calming effect of nicotine helps to soothe his nerves, thereby reducing his pain. Only he knows. He still shaves blindly, because he can't see below his nose without moving his head down and of course you can't do that when you're shaving! Fair enough, he's looking in the mirror, but when he shaves, he has to take his glasses off, and then he can't see anyhow! I wonder if I've explained this the way he would? I don't expect so—all I know is he can't see what he's doing when he shaves!

The next doctor's appointment is in mid-May, at which time they will probably send him for his second MRI, so I hope we can now start getting back to normality. It's been an arduous road, but we've learned a lot through it. Craig is alive and well, and that surely is a miracle.

Tuesday, 24 March 2009—Email

For the past two months Craig has been doing well, and although his vision is still limited, he can do the work he was doing before. He lost his job in Johannesburg because he couldn't drive, and it's a long way from where he lives. In the last month or so, he's been working for the same boss, Loraine, who owns a few printer ink shops, including one in Benoni. Craig has been standing in for someone who's on leave, and because it's close by, Georgie takes him there daily and collects him in the afternoons. Loraine and her mother, Marie, have been praying for him since his headaches first started and have been of great encouragement. After much haggling with his insurance company, he managed to get a full pay-out on a disability policy that he had, and he now has enough money to buy one of Loraine's shops. This is good news because he can do the same job, which he's very good at, and the shop will be his own. I knew something good would come out of this. The deal will probably go through around June this year. Oh, and I've just found out that he's been driving his car. I'm told that he's found a back route to Alberton, where his new shop is located, and he's planning on driving himself to work daily. I don't even want to think about it. But he's not a child; I'm just the mother, and mothers are neurotic!

Brian is well, and things have improved since his back operation. It was a slow process, but everything seems to be working normally again. He's back at the gym and riding his bike in national races. He did very well in the Cape Argus a couple of weeks ago.

As for Ian and me, we are well. Ian continues to pursue his hobby and is once again South African champion in the expert class of large scale model aerobatics. He's working relentlessly in the model aircraft shop in Woodmead, and I'm beginning to wonder if he'll ever be able to retire for the second time. Today I received my ten-year long service award in my son Doug's business, having graduated from PA to HR manager a couple of years ago. The business has grown extensively since I've been there. We now have franchisees around the country, and our head office staff has trebled. I told them the reason I've stayed so long is to keep an eye on my eldest little boy, who is also six feet two inches tall and forty-seven years old. I'm running two Weigh-Less classes a week and am taking lessons in quilting, having tired of dressmaking after a few decades. Life is never boring around here.

Even though to all intents and purposes things are running smoothly as far as Craig's health is concerned, there's an ever-present undertone pulling our thoughts back to the actuality of that beast inside his head. Every plan or decision I make revolves around when he might need my help. Right now I believe he's safe, so I've made plans to go to England for a few weeks to visit Debbie and the grandchildren. After all these years of marriage to Ian, I've come to the point where I no longer try to persuade him to come with me. If I want to see my girls, I have to go alone. I'll be leaving at the end of March and will be back towards the end of April.

Saturday, 23 May 2009

I treasured every minute with my English family, and was home again all too soon. No wheels fell off the bus while I was away, proving once again that I'm not indispensable! It was straight back to work, catching up with home affairs, and all the extras that lend themselves to never a dull moment.

Craig's visit to the neurosurgeon last week proved to be a fruitless occurrence, with a new doctor who knew nothing about his case. The doctor told Craig he didn't need an MRI at this time and should book one for January next year. This is ludicrous, considering the fact that the tumour has never been properly identified. By the time January comes, it will be a whole year since any kind of scan was done. I'm really angry about this because I'm convinced that the tumour should be examined sooner. But they are the ones who call the tune. In my opinion, there are some doctors in that hospital who don't know what they're doing.

Since my return from England, I've had a lot of backache, as well as arthritic pains in my hips. Having had a hip replacement six years ago, I decided it was time to get the other hip fixed, so I visited my orthopaedic surgeon, who hit me with the shocking news that the one I'd already had done had slipped and would have to be done again. After contemplation, I sought a second opinion from a world-class surgeon, who agreed that I needed a revision hip replacement, but added that there were other complications, including the necessity for a bone graft to the pelvis and some extensive muscle repair. All this came as a huge shock, but I accept that surgery cannot be avoided. I've made a decision to change my doctor, and arrangements are under way. I'm telling myself to be unruffled about this, but I think I'll have to speak louder. Right now surgery and a long haul on crutches are not the most appealing thoughts in my mind. Nevertheless, the operation is scheduled for 1 September. I'll be hospitalized for ten days and on crutches for three months, about twice as long as a straightforward hip replacement.

July 2009

Craig is fine, or if he isn't, he doesn't say anything about it. His business isn't doing too badly, considering the recession. There's no change to his eyesight, but he's able to do his job, and is very grateful for that. Despite my reservations about his visual capabilities, he's driving to work each day. I suppose I should count my blessings in the knowledge that he doesn't drive on the motorway.

One of Georgie's daughters was married this month, and Craig gave her away. He looked well and very smart in his dress suit. It's often difficult to comprehend that he still has a foreign body in his head, but the fundamental uncertainty of it is a constant that cannot be ignored. He's trying hard to have fun, like everyone else, but it scares me when I see him with a Bacardi, or a can of beer in one hand, and a cigarette in the other. I daren't say a word though, because I know I'll be told that he's the only one who can decide how he should deal with his affliction. He's right, of course.

July 2009

Tuesday, 15 September 2009—Email

What a bonus my op turned out to be, a great success, to be sure! There are a few small snags, but I'm doing well. I did appreciate the luxury of a private clinic. The food was so good that I asked the chef for a couple of recipes. Ian took two weeks off work to look after me. I have to say I am a very fortunate woman to be married to a man who is able to do an amazing turnaround and take on the role of nurse without any effort whatsoever! He can cook so well that I've decided never to venture into the kitchen again!

It saddens me when I think about my son having to go to a state hospital. He never thought that belonging to a medical aid scheme was necessary, but I know he wishes he had now. Nonetheless, he's grateful for having been accepted at The Hospital, which is recognised as being one of South Africa's foremost public health institutions. It's by no means perfect, but it is better than most. Generally, state hospitals in South Africa leave more than a lot to be desired; in fact, some of them are absolutely shocking, as I've said before. One only has to look at the media, the television, and the newspapers. They continually publicise the outrage that goes on in the state hospitals; yet no one does anything about it. I recently read a report that said that doctors are being forced to put patients' lives at risk; I can add that we are experiencing this ourselves. But we are lucky; we haven't experienced the worst of it. There's always something for which to be thankful.

Chapter 8

Sunday, 17 January 2010

For almost a year Craig has been reasonably well, and even though he has been aware that a portion of the tumour is still there, he's been leading a fairly normal life. He has managed significantly well with his partial vision and has been running his business single-handedly. In October I thanked the Lord again that I could share another birthday with my son.

The sad news is that the tumour is back with a vengeance. In December he came down with the same symptoms he had before his seizure in October 2008, when he was admitted to hospital and we almost lost him. The past week has been a difficult time. We scheduled an appointment for a routine MRI scan for the beginning of January, but the MRI machine had broken down. That was when the drama began. I'm still convinced that this scan should have been done months ago. Craig's condition is serious, so some bright spark suggested we take him to another hospital, also one of South Africa's huge training centres, purported to be the largest hospital in the world. I've learned enough about state hospitals in the past two years to know that one cannot simply go there and expect results, so I diligently phoned their MRI department to enquire as to whether the scan could be done there.

"Oh yes," declared the gentlemen whose name I stupidly did not write down, "All you need to do is get a referral from one of the doctors at The Hospital, bring it here, and we'll do the job."

What luck, but oh my word, never believe anything a government official tells you over the phone! We rushed to The Hospital, fought for an appointment, sat in a half-day queue, and finally got to see an Afrikaans neurosurgeon, who admitted he'd never heard this one before, but willingly wrote a letter, stating that Craig's case was critically urgent and asking if they would please do an MRI. I had no idea where to go, so Ian took a day's leave from work and off the three of us went. That place is hugely huge. An Internet site claims it occupies 173 acres of ground. It's made up of buildings all over the place, so while Ian went off to find a parking area, Craig and I made our baffled way into the complex, looking for signs to direct us to the MRI department. What an adventure! Ian, in the meantime, parked the car and started out on an expedition to find us. Even with the use of cell phones, this took a long time. Craig was not well at all and was lagging behind me, desperately hoping that we were not going to tour the whole premises. We meandered through a maze of concrete pathways, following arrows that seemed to point in circles. I told Craig to wait by a certain pole, because he was threatening to pass out.

"I'll come back for you when I find the place," I said, hoping I wasn't being too optimistic.

Along the way, I saw all sorts of shocking sights, such as shot people being wheeled in on gurneys with blood everywhere and dead bodies that weren't even covered. I didn't want to ask anyone for directions because I doubted they'd be particularly interested in me, especially if they were dead. In due course I met up with Craig and Ian right outside the MRI department. Ian had picked Craig up en route. The waiting room was almost deserted, expect for one old man spewing blood all over the dilapidated bed on which he was lying.

"I don't like this place," I said to Ian, "I think I'm going to be sick."

"Not a good idea," Craig chipped in, "There's no one to wipe it up."

An open door led into an office, behind which was an empty MRI machine. We walked into the office because there was nothing to say we shouldn't, but we did get a couple of weird looks from the occupants, who were apparently radiographers and radiologists. One person came to assist us, and I gave her the referral letter, explaining our desperate circumstances. She gave it to someone else, who read it without looking up and handed it back to her, shaking his head.

"Sorry," she said. "We're not some place you can walk into without an appointment. Besides, you don't belong in this hospital."

We tried to explain how we came to be there, on the recommendation of one of their staff members, whose name we did not know, but who'd promised we could get the scans done there. What a joke! The woman was cold at first, but when she saw that I was almost in tears, she took Craig's previous scans, looked them up and down, and informed us that this wasn't a serious tumour, there was no cause for concern, and no harm would come to him while we waited for the machine at The Hospital to be repaired. What a thoughtless assumption! She had no idea about anything at all.

I've never seen so much disappointment on a person's face as I saw on Craig's that day. It was as though all hope had flown out the window. We retreated like a troop of hopeless tramps. There was nothing to say. Chicken Little must have felt like that when the sky fell down. But of course the sky didn't really fall down; it was just an acorn. Perhaps that's how I should have viewed the situation. It felt as though the sky had fallen down, but in reality there was no damage at all. Things might have become very complicated if the scans had been done at another hospital.

It wasn't meant to be. We dropped Craig off at his house and silently drove home, like a couple of deflated balloons. I lay awake all night, wondering how Craig was doing and what he'd done to deserve this.

The MRI machine at The Hospital was fixed a few days later, and the scans were done, but not without hours of waiting once again. Did I mention that the toilets are clean in that section of the hospital? Bonus time!

Friday was neurosurgical clinic day, with the customary long wait before we saw our friend the Indian doctor, who says Craig will have to have another operation, as the tumour is substantially larger than it was, and is now affecting a different part of his brain. This was devastating news, but did not surprise Craig, who'd been saying all along that something was radically wrong. He kept on telling me that it felt as though someone had parked a Boeing inside his head. I am getting "furiouser and furiouser", as Alice might have said, that the scans weren't done months ago, but there's no point in agonising. The only thing that could change Africa would be for Atlantis to rise up from the sea, and that's not about to happen. The drawback now—wait for it—is that there are no beds available. The neurosurgical ward only has twenty-two beds, and there are hundreds of patients on the waiting list. In fact, I was told that some patients have been waiting a year to have surgery. The surgeon told us that this operation is urgent, but that there wasn't much he could do about the waiting list.

"The only thing I can suggest," he told us, "is that you take a walk up to the neuro ward and chat to the sister about getting a bed."

"Are you telling me," I responded, "that we have more influence than you do?"

He laughed. "Truthfully, yes. I've got Craig on the priority list, but there are hundreds of priority patients. Whereas if *you*," he was looking at me, "go into the ward and tell them I sent you, they might give you real priority!"

I sat there with my mouth open.

The surgeon grinned. "I don't know how they function, Ma'am, but if they like you . . ." He was looking at my open mouth. "Ah, just go and try. Your son needs this surgery. I think you will make it happen!"

All I could say was, "Right!"

"Oh, and rest assured," he continued, "that I am planning on doing this surgery myself, and I will make sure that there's a pathologist in the theatre. I will personally ensure that he takes the specimen to the lab for testing. We will not have a repeat of the last histology antics."

Down to Green Block we traipsed, and then up to the sixth floor; Mother Hen on her crutch, and blind Bartimaeus tagging behind. I often wondered if that crutch gained me any sympathy. Goody, goody, the nursing sister on duty was one with whom I was familiar, so I buttered her up by telling her how pretty she looked (or some such remark) and we became friends. As usual, Craig was silent. I could see that the ward was full to overflowing, but I told her what the surgeon had said about urgency.

"We have two hundred waiting for beds," she said, "but if you phone me every day, I'll see what I can do."

I didn't understand how that would work. "What about the two hundred?"

"First come, first served," she remarked.

I still didn't understand.

"Keep phoning, Mrs Craig," she said. "If you should phone while anyone is being discharged, your son will get the bed."

I was incredulous. "You'll get sick of the sound of my voice," I told her.

"No, I won't," she smiled. "I want to help Gentleman Craig."

Having said all this, the frightening truth is that conditions at The Hospital are horrifying. I imagine it would be hard for my readers outside Africa to realise the enormity of this reality. Below is an extract from an article, which appeared in a leading South African newspaper a few months ago:

Backlog at Top Hospital

> A total of 1567 patients are awaiting surgery, because of staff shortages and high volumes. Only priority 1 and 2 patients will be seen at this hospital. These are patients in need of emergency specialist medical care, i.e. life threatening within 2 hours, which cannot be rendered at the regional or district hospital, the clinic or the medical practitioner.

Only a miracle will secure Craig a space for the urgent surgery he needs.

As for me, I've recuperated well from my surgery and am hoping that by the end of this month I can discard my second crutch. On 29 November last year I wrote in my journal that I was very frustrated with having been on two crutches for three months, and that having to be dependent on others had brought me down a peg or two. I was wondering if God was trying to teach me something, but wasn't sure what it was—humility perhaps, and a better understanding of the impediments allotted to disabled persons. Who knows? But I do have a better understanding now, and maybe I'm better equipped to deal with whatever is in store for Craig. I've been on either one crutch or two for almost six months, and I'm tired of it. My hip is fine. The pelvic bone graft apparently takes about nine months to set properly, so I still have to be careful. My surgeon also tried to repair my leg muscle that had been damaged during the previous surgery, and I'm not sure about the state of that yet. I still limp when I walk without crutches, but I'm madly hoping that will go in time. I don't think my limp is as bad as it was before. Cavorting around that hospital on Friday was a test for me because once again we were there for seven hours, plus two hours travelling time, so I was worn out when I got home.

Craig has just phoned me—he's not doing well at all. That Boeing inside his head is about to take off.

Saturday, 30 January 2010—Email

I've been nervous over the past couple of weeks. I've certainly had bad days, but I end up kicking myself when I feel my faith level dropping, because God has done so much in our lives, and I know that trusting Him is the only way to go.

Despite the long waiting list, Craig was admitted on Friday last week (22 January). That sister wasn't joking. I've seen many folks in those wards who lie there, using up valuable beds, endlessly waiting to get an MRI, or to get a place in the theatre for their surgery. That's what happened to Craig a year ago, before his first operation. There was a man in his ward who had been there for a week, waiting for a scan. He was walking around on crutches due to a back ailment, but wasn't seriously ill, yet he had a bed in a place where many people die before they can get into a hospital—and that is the truth. On the day that Craig left there, that man was still waiting for his MRI.

On Sunday evening Craig was assessed, given all the necessary prelim tests, chest X-rays, and so forth. An anaesthetist visited him to tell him they would operate the next day—only two days after he arrived there, but on Monday morning (the twenty-fifth) he was greeted with the news that he might not have the op that day because there were two ahead of him, which could take a long time. "Here we go again" was starting to become a common phrase in my vocabulary, but "What do you know?" occasionally featured as well. One of the ops was cancelled, and Craig was in the theatre by 9:30 a.m. The Hospital is starting to live up to its alleged reputation of being the best government hospital in the country. Since the last time he was there, the wards have been painted and everything is clean, probably because the World Cup football tournament will be played in South Africa soon, and they could be expecting some casualties, or international journalists, or both. But whatever the reason, it's great news. We have every confidence in the surgeons, and our perception of the nursing staff has been good. Unfortunately, there is still administrative chaos, a huge shortage of beds, and when you do get a bed you often have to bring your own bed linen. Some of the things that go on there are preposterous, which is why I call every good thing that happens to our son a miracle.

He was remarkably cheerful when he emerged from the theatre, after a four-and-a-half-hour operation. As planned, a pathologist was present during surgery, and we were told that he personally took the specimen to the laboratory for analysis. After surgery, Craig was admitted to ICU, where he remained until Thursday the twenty-eighth. From there he went straight home, having been there for less than a week all told. When he told me to come and fetch him, I didn't believe they had discharged him, so I phoned the ward sister to ask if he was telling the truth. He is now at home and doing well. In fact, when I spoke to him this morning, he said he was bored and wanted to go back to work. I asked him if I could fetch him so he could spend the day at our house, and he said he wasn't *that* bored! Cheeky so and so! Georgie's working in the shop, so he's alone at home, but he's so healthy that I'm confident he'll be all right. On Friday next week I'll be taking him to see a surgeon to have his clips removed.

Once again the surgeons were not able to remove the whole tumour. They say it doesn't look malignant, but they don't know why it's growing so fast. He'll probably have to have radiation, depending on the histology results. So it's still a waiting game.

Sunday, 7 February 2010—Email

It may have appeared that this year got off to a bad start for this family, but my philosophy is that within every negative situation there is a positive. Countless times that has been true for us. Since this ordeal started, we've faced complications galore. Nasty little voices have crept into my head, suggesting that I accept mediocrity and settle for whatever comes our way. I've learned never to listen to those nasty voices.

On Friday, 5 February 2010, I took Craig to the clinic for a post-op check-up and to have the clips taken out of his head. That sounds pretty simple, doesn't it? In a First World country it probably would be. I left my home at 6:00 a.m. and walked through my front door eleven hours later, at 5:00 p.m., nine hours of which were in the hospital—which beat even the last visit, which was a total of nine hours including travelling time.

After a two-and-a-half-hour wait, we saw a neurosurgeon, one we have never seen before. The nasty voice said, "Hmph, he won't know anything about this case, blah blah." Well, he did! He told us there were no histology results yet, but Craig must have the clips out, a blood test must be done, and an MRI booking should be made for this coming week. Ha! Ha! Getting an MRI booking is a performance, to say the least. The surgeon told us that regardless of whether or not the tumour proved to be malignant, radiation therapy was imperative because of the rapid growth rate, so another MRI was essential.

So off we go. Clips are removed without even having to wait, but they won't do the blood test because the documentation is incorrect and only the doctor can change it. Now the doctors are all in consultation and the queue is long, but old Mother

Hen here isn't having any of this! I've gotten that place down to a fine art—don't think there's anything I will not attempt to conquer! I march into the nurses' station and (politely, because you have to) request to see the doctor. I'm basically told to continue marching into his consulting room! Being the courteous person I am, I decide to wait till the current patient comes out of there, then I jump the queue, which I was told to do, so I'm not out of line (excuse the pun!). My son stands back and doesn't want to know my name!

What do you know ? In the consulting room I find that doctor, as well as the young woman surgeon who assisted with the surgery. What good fortune! We all have a friendly natter and they fix the documentation, so off we go again and the blood test is done. A long walk to radiology ensues. What a surprise—they are fully booked, and we can't get an appointment for an MRI. We insist that it's urgent, so they contact the doctor by telephone. We are then asked if we would be able to come on a Sunday, as it's the only way they can fit us in. Favour again. So the appointment is for Sunday, 21 February, the soonest they can do it. It's a miracle.

Now that we have to wait a couple of weeks, we realise that Craig doesn't have enough medication to last until then, so we need a prescription from the doctor. Craig wants to go home, but when Mother Hen is on the rampage, she is in charge of her thirty-eight-year-old son! He says he's got sufficient medication, but I say it's the wrong stuff, so I insist on going back to the clinic, which means I have to intrude on the doctors again. I see the lady surgeon, whose name I can't pronounce, walking down the passage. I call out, "Doctor . . .", while Craig hides his face! He should know by now that I can and will do whatever it takes. The lady surgeon says we must get Craig's file and come to her consulting room, which we do, respectfully waiting for her to finish with her last patient of the day, because it's now quite late, and I suspect the entire staff has "gone to lunch". Whilst we are waiting, another neurosurgeon spots Craig and comes to chat with us. This never happens—but it did! Craig cringes again when I ask the doctor to write down the lady surgeon's name for me. He does so and tells us not to sue her! This probably all sounds silly, but my, how it lightens up a long stressful day! The lady comes out and writes the prescription after consulting with the head neurosurgeon, who performed the first operation. She's a young intern, and she calls him "Sir". My friend the Indian surgeon performed this operation and she assisted. The Indian man is one of the top surgeons.

The lady surgeon was about to leave when she asked, "Has anyone taken the trouble to find out if the results are back from the lab?"

The answer was no. She asked us to wait a few more minutes while she went to the lab to check. I got a dreamlike feeling that we'd been down this road before! Craig took the script to the pharmacy, and of course we waited another three hours for that to be filled. In the meantime, the lady came back carrying the report! If we hadn't had all the foregoing delays, we would not have received that report, and who knows, it might have gone missing again before our next visit. My readers will know by now that I am not joking.

I cannot expound on how I felt when I saw that paper in her hand. We've waited fifteen months to find out whether or not the tumour is malignant.

"You are so precious," I told the lady, and she looked so amazed by my accolade that I felt driven to tell her that my son had said she was the nicest doctor there and that everyone liked her.

"Now you can tell me the results," I said. She was visibly touched and sat next to me to explain the report, which was two pages long and full of very, very, *very* long words. She said that no cancer had been detected, and the tumour was of a benign nature, but still had to be shrunk because it was not slow-growing, as they had originally thought. For a moment it struck me as odd that the tumour could be benign but "not slow-growing," That would suggest that it was *fast*-growing, in which case, surely it must be malignant? I'm not a brain surgeon, so I didn't contemplate that thought for long. I was content with being over the moon that there was no cancer. Craig came back and all I said to him was, "It's not cancer," and all he said was, "Phew!" We had quite a long chat with the lady surgeon, who wasn't in any hurry—what a lovely human being. But I was to learn that she, too, had some lessons to learn. What I did know, even as she spoke, was that benign tumours can still kill you, and this one could not be removed in its entirety through surgery.

We drove home that day with a sense of relief, although the fundamental truth was that there still remained an element of uncertainty about the situation.

Sunday, 21 February 2010

I took Craig for his MRI this morning. It would be great if one could always go on a Sunday—no traffic and not much waiting. With any luck we are now on the last lap of all these high jinks.

Meanwhile, to make our lives a tad more complicated, I have a recently-detected lung disease, which I've supposedly had since childhood. Lately, it has become a hindrance. The doctors have decided to call it bronchiectasis, which could have been caused by measles (or something) when I was a child. Because it wasn't treated, it has now decided to show its ugly head, causing me to get a peculiar cough and sore chest. I was instructed to use a cortisone inhaler for the next six months, but had a nasty reaction to it and am worse than I was before. I've had enough of doctors!

Chapter 9

The day 28 February 2010 brought with it a major shock. The tumour *is* malignant. That day the consultant was a soft-spoken, wheelchair-bound, Congolese neurosurgeon. We were later told by a patient that he'd been hijacked, a common occurrence in South Africa. He was shot in the back, paralysing his spinal cord. We all have a story to tell.

In his distinctly French accent, the surgeon explained that brain malignancies are not the same as malignancies elsewhere in the body. Perhaps that was why the young lady surgeon told us Craig's tumour wasn't cancerous. If a brain tumour is classified *benign*, this usually means it's non-life-threatening. However, in the brain, if a tumour is not cancerous it can still be considered *malignant*. Basically, malignancy depends on what structures of the brain are affected and how difficult it is to treat the tumour.

We were told that Craig has a glioblastoma multiforme (GBM) tumour, the most aggressive type of malignant brain tumour that exists. Life expectancy for those who have it is less than one year. The surgeon explained that tumours can change from benign to malignant, so it was possible that this tumour started off as a slow-growing one, but later became malignant. I subsequently read on an Internet website that although the percentage is low, certain GBM tumours "may have evolved from a low-grade astrocytoma," which is a benign tumour.

Although Craig's tumour is deemed to be a primary GBM, we cannot ignore the fact that over a year elapsed between the first surgical removal, after which the biopsy results were lost, and the second, when a biopsy confirmed his GBM status. It is quite possible, in fact probable, that it was originally a grade four astrocytoma. Although this phenomenon represents less than ten per cent of GBM cases, it is more common in younger patients, meaning those under forty. Nevertheless, the prognosis is bad, the average survival time being under nine months after surgical removal of most of the tumour, followed by radiation. The extremely infiltrative nature of this tumour makes complete surgical removal impossible, and long-term survival of over five years is achieved by less than three per cent of those afflicted. So whatever this tumour was, or is now, the prospects are not good. Our disbelief must have been evident to the neurosurgeon. He looked at his patient empathetically.

"Do you pray?" he asked.

Craig smiled, "Oh yes. That's the reason I've survived two major brain operations."

I nodded in agreement.

"Don't stop praying," the doctor said, "You have a very serious condition. According to the law of averages, you shouldn't be alive right now. You're entirely in God's hands."

"That's a good place to be," I remember saying, but I don't remember much else.

I know that the surgeon told us about some form of chemotherapy that could be used on GBM tumours, but it was extremely expensive and not available in state hospitals in South Africa. He went on to say that even medical aid schemes were reluctant to pay for it because the rate of success was zero. Clinical studies showed no benefit from chemotherapy in cases of GBM tumours.

"Some wealthy patients have been known to demand it as a last resort," he told us, "but to my knowledge, it has never saved a life."

The doctor spoke so softly that it was difficult to grasp all that he was saying, and I don't think Craig was listening at all. He did ask me a lot of questions afterwards. I think he used to think that I was Mrs Mastermind, ever able to comprehend the entire hypothesis of neurosurgical terminology, whatever that means.

"Don't give up," the surgeon was saying, "There is light at the end of the tunnel. I'm referring you to radiation oncology." He picked up the phone, spoke softly for a minute, then turned to Craig and said, "You can go down there right now. They're on the fourth floor, Orange Block. Here's you referral."

I put out my hand to shake his. "Thank you, Doctor."

His lips smiled, but his eyes told a different story. I was learning quickly to read the eyes of doctors.

Of course, we had to wait again. We didn't talk much that day. First we had to get another new file, and then we sat in a large waiting room where everyone looked miserable—as though they'd been waiting there all day. What a surprise! One thing that I did notice was that the place was immaculately clean. The floors actually shone. At last we got to the place in the queue where you move up, chair by chair, getting closer to the door behind which sat the radiation oncologist, a pretty Asian lady, who greeted us with a broad smile. As she began to explain the intricacies of the tumour, I noticed that she kept using the word "cancer". I had to stop her, much to Craig's indignation.

"If I understood the neurosurgeon correctly," I said, "he intimated malignancy, but not cancer."

At first, she looked a little puzzled, and then she said, "Neurosurgeons and oncologists sometimes have a different perception of what is cancer and what is not. As far as we're concerned, anything that's malignant is cancer. This tumour is galloping. I'm really sorry, but it is cancer." She must have noticed that Craig was looking confused. "It doesn't really matter what you call it," she said kindly, "The fact is that it's very dangerous, and it's going to kill you if we don't try to remove it."

She went on to explain that GBM's do not spread to the rest of the body as other cancers do, and can shrink with radiation. They are particularly harmful because they can damage vital parts of the brain. Although radiotherapy rarely cures glioblastoma, studies show that it can double the average survival rate of patients. Various tests had to be done prior to radiation, including liver and HIV. A face mask would be made, to ensure that Craig's head doesn't move during the procedure, and this would be strapped to his head and bolted to the table during the six to seven week course of daily radiation.

Wednesday, 3 March 2010—Email

The radiation oncologist phoned Craig this morning, and other staff members phoned him many times. He was supposed to go for a consultation on Thursday next week, but it's been cancelled because this is too urgent. Now he has to go in on Friday at 7:00 a.m. to get the face mask made. There's so much to think about. Craig worries about his business, which, not surprisingly, is taking a bit of a knock.

To make matters worse, last night I had terrible chest pains all night. I paid my GP a visit this morning, and had an ECG. My heart's fine. I had more lung X-rays, which proved there's no change. Now they think it might be pneumonia, so I'm on antibiotics, but I'm still in a lot of pain. I want to be there on Friday, so I'm stressing a bit, which is probably why I got sick in the first place. Come hell or high water, I *will* be at the hospital on Friday.

Friday, 5 March 2010

This morning I was feeling much better and managed to drive to the hospital without any effort. We collected Craig's file and proceeded to the planning section of radiation oncology. From there we were directed to the mould room. Two smiling ladies were there to welcome Craig and start making the face mask.

There was no waiting, and the procedure took less than ten minutes. It's an interesting technique, which they invited me to observe. They raised no objection to Craig's request for me to take photos with my mobile phone. It was a strange feeling to be clicking away in a medical environment where my son was the patient, but good to be able to share the experience with the rest of the family later on. For Craig, the process was a little claustrophobic, but he didn't seem to mind. First, they covered his face and hair with cling film to protect them from the mould mixture, leaving a hole for his nose so that he could breathe. Bandages were used to make a plaster of Paris cast around his head. He ended up resembling the Frankenstein monster! After about five minutes, the plaster of Paris had set and the mould was taken off. A Perspex mask will be made from this mould, and this will be used during the radiation treatment. Next Friday they'll strap the mask to his face and do a CT scan, to see exactly where they have to aim the radiation beams. Technology is amazing. He's not allowed to cut his hair, because the mask must fit exactly as the mould was made today.

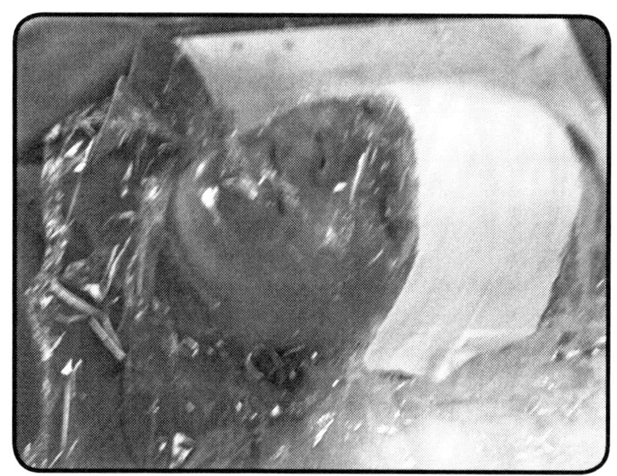

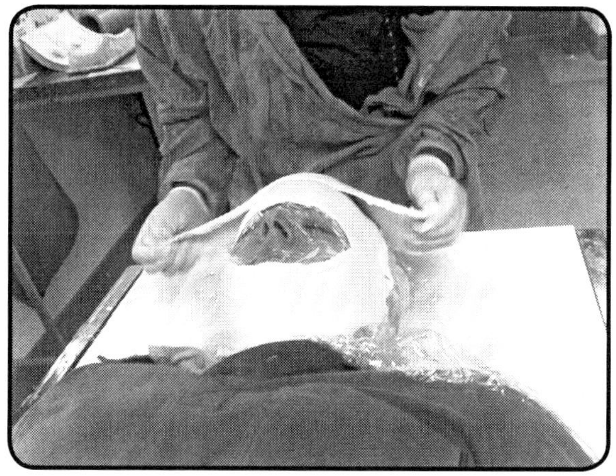

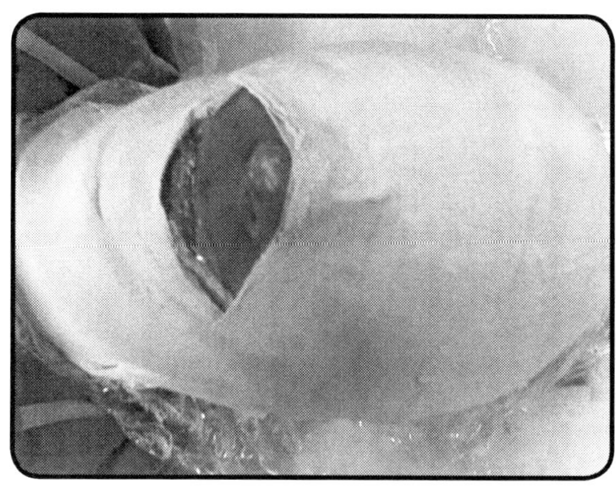

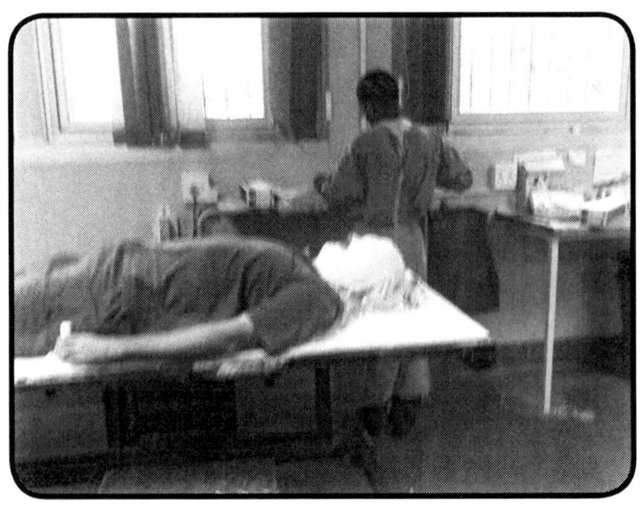

Making the cast for the face mask

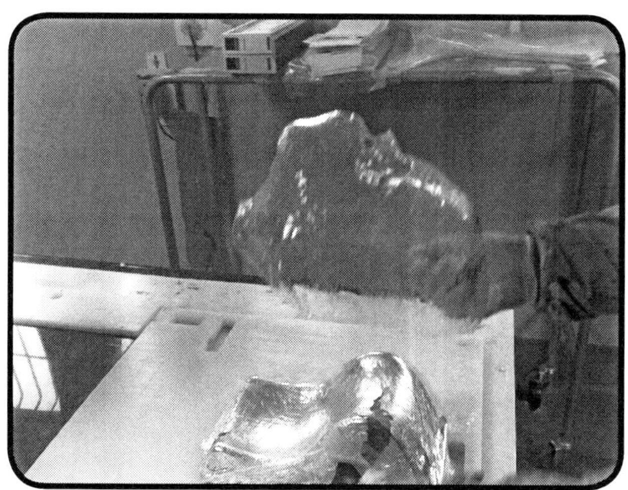

Sample of completed Perspex face mask

I'm very proud of my boy. He's as positive as ever, and many times he handles the situation a lot better than I do. But he's the world's worst back seat driver! I think the way I drive in heavy traffic is quite staggering! One has to be a rocket scientist to figure out what the taxi drivers in that city are going to do next. These individuals are a unique breed of road hog; their so-called minibus "taxis" form the local public transport system, used mainly by commuters to and from their workplaces. They run without timetables, without regard for other drivers, and many times without brakes. They duck and dive in heavy traffic, repeatedly stopping to offload passengers. They push other vehicles off the road, make third lanes in two-lane traffic, and find many creative ways to break the rules of the road. Once, in heavy rain, Ian and I saw a taxi speeding along the island that separated a dual carriageway in order to reach the traffic lights before anyone else did! In so doing, the driver bumped and bent a sturdy street light, but remained undaunted, continuing his journey to accomplish his mission.

The Hospital is the hardest place in the world to navigate from Benoni if you don't know the route. But I'm a driving genius, even if Craig doesn't seem to think so. He moans and groans the whole way there and back.

"Mom, you're going to hit that car. Mom you're in the wrong lane. Mom, I've got a brain tumour; I don't want to die in a car crash!"

I tell him it's astounding how he can see so well on the road, and yet he bumps into people in the shops and struggles to buy a loaf of bread. The irony is that what I'm saying is true, but he can joke about it. Ah yes, we need a little giggle, but can still get mad at one another, like normal people.

Friday, 19 March 2010

Nought but a classic cliché can say what I want to say now: It never rains, it pours! I had a midnight crisis with my own health, culminating in my being admitted to hospital the next day. I was discharged after ten frightening days. My lungs felt as though they were being spiked with a pitchfork, the end result of which was a nasty lung biopsy, which was undeniably worse than any hip replacement that I've had. I'm at home in bed at the moment and can barely move.

Beneath a tight bandage, I discovered fourteen metal clips under my left breast. I previously had no idea how big the cut was. I'm convinced they've injured my ribs and that I am much worse now than I was before I was hospitalized. I suppose bed rest will fix this, but I'm highly annoyed because the conclusion was that they couldn't find anything, so have called my malady a "bug". That's right, blame the bugs again! The treatment I received in a private hospital was atrocious, and I'm exasperated.

Craig had to take himself to the hospital today, which accentuated my own stress levels, but everything went well. Last week Ian took him there, but the CT scanner was broken (again!), so that was a waste of time. They have now finished making the face mask, as well as a body cast, which is attached to the face mask so that he cannot move at all whilst undergoing radiation therapy. He continues to amaze everyone, taking it all in his stride. Doug and Lindy are away on holiday, and Brian left for the States on business this morning, so Ian and I are plodding along on our own.

As some literary fellow once said, "All's well that ends well," so let's hope it ends soon!

Tuesday, 30 March 2010

My clips have been removed, and I'm feeling slightly more comfortable, but still not well. What a performance! I've been to the office a couple of times, albeit feeling weak and woozy, but the work was piling up, and I consider myself a martyr! I see the proverbial quack next week—I say quack because I'm so fed up with doctors—the two I'm with at the moment are not on the same page, and my confusion increases. The bronchiectasis covers both my lungs, but has never before caused a setback. They tell me now I have contracted some wretched bug with a long name, and this has superimposed itself on the bronchiectasis, which disrupts my whole system. I'm not sure I believe any of it. It simply confirms my guinea pig status. My antibiotics were finished this morning, but the original chest pain I had in the beginning is still there, so I give up!

Monday, 12 April 2010

My chest woes have subsided, and now it's Craig's turn. I received a distress call from him last night. There are times when I think he merely wants to talk to someone because he's feeling rotten. That ugly tumour is giving him a hard time again, and he says he feels as though someone has inflated a balloon in his head. It's especially bad when he lies down. This is seriously disturbing him now. I told him I'd be phoning the hospital today, and although he objected a bit, I know that's what he wanted me to do. I feel so helpless when he phones me like that, wishing I could take his place. I have *so* had enough of this.

I did phone the oncology department this morning, and the response was better than last time. They intimated that they would phone when they were ready for him, but then went on to say that it would be sometime this week, so I hope that's the truth. I told the woman I spoke to that he's in trouble and she reiterated that they would phone him this week. Craig's got all sorts of theories that aren't very constructive, but I reckon it's nerves. I'd be nervous. I told him I want this to be over before the Soccer World Cup starts, so we don't have to get caught up in the traffic going for daily radiation, but he maintains there won't be any traffic—they'll all be at the football! We can still laugh a bit. On reflection, I don't care about the World Cup; I just want my son fixed.

Chapter 10

I suppose one would call it autumn in this country now. We don't have four equal seasons because we tend to go straight from summer into winter, with perhaps a month in between when the leaves fall off the trees, so I guess that's autumn. Our garden has many trees, so the ground is constantly covered in leaves, and we spend hours sweeping them up at this time of the year. The weather's nice though—not too hot and not too cold. I love watching the seasons change through the big glass windows in our sun lounge. I spend a lot of time with God in that room. Lately I've been talking to Him about seasonal changes in our lives. I think that just as He created the sun and the moon and the stars and the earth and got them to work in conjunction with one another to form the seasons, so He created seasons for our lives. He gave us choices, and the choices we make determine how we cope with our spiritual seasons. Whichever way you look at it, autumn is the forerunner of winter, that cold, uncomfortable time when we feel as though the sun is taking forever to appear in the sky. Winter presents some challenges, but thankfully encompasses the ever-present hope of spring and the guarantee of summer to follow. Yes, it's autumn now, and the leaves are slowly falling, but we still have a little time before the cold weather arrives.

Friday, 16 April 2010—Email

Under the impression that they were going to start the radiation today, off we went to the hospital, but it turned out they still have to do certain planning and mapping of Craig's head, in order to ensure that the radiotherapy is aimed precisely at the cancer. This certainly is a complex procedure.

After waiting four hours on an uncomfortable seat (we did manage to sneak down to the canteen for half an hour to have some tea and a bite to eat), Craig at long last got in to have the mapping done. They call the machine a simulator. Well then, I do want to see the real thing. It's difficult to explain, but there are beams all over the place, computers, loads and loads of numbers coming up on screens, and "what what what", as the African nationals tend to say. The beams have to intersect in certain places to pinpoint the affected areas. All the time Craig lay on his stomach, face in the mask and chest on the body cast, which he fits into exactly, arms by his side. Poor fellow, he had to remain in that pose for another half hour after I was asked to leave so they could take X-rays. Another wait ensued, but I'm sorry to say that the radiographers were not happy with the X-rays, and we were told that when they are not happy, the doctor is usually unhappy as well, in which case the procedure will have to be done all over again. He may need a retake, and if not, he may be able to start radiation, which must be done for at least three consecutive days before the weekend break. We have another public holiday coming up soon, so that may also affect the planning. Here we go again! However, I am relieved that something is happening at last.

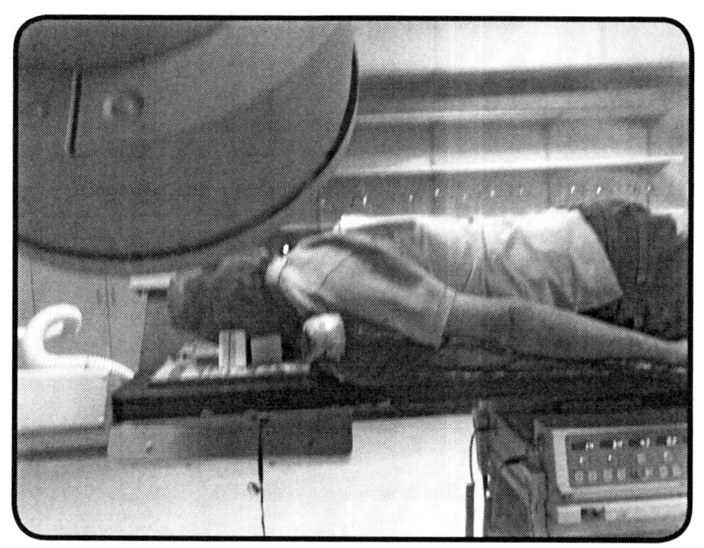

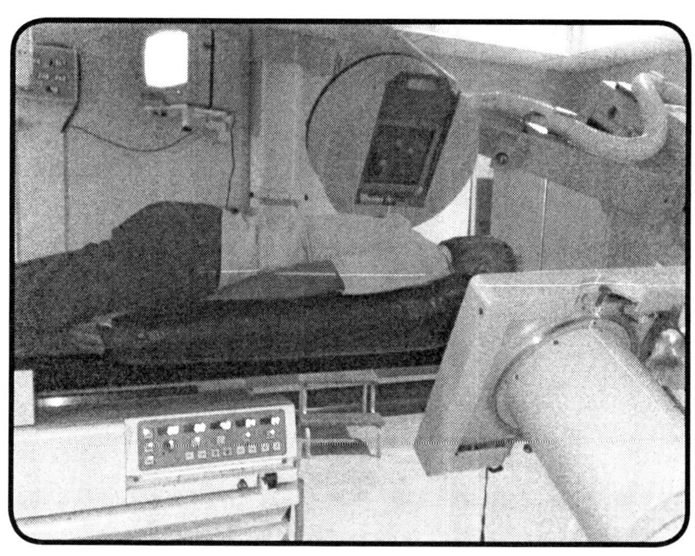

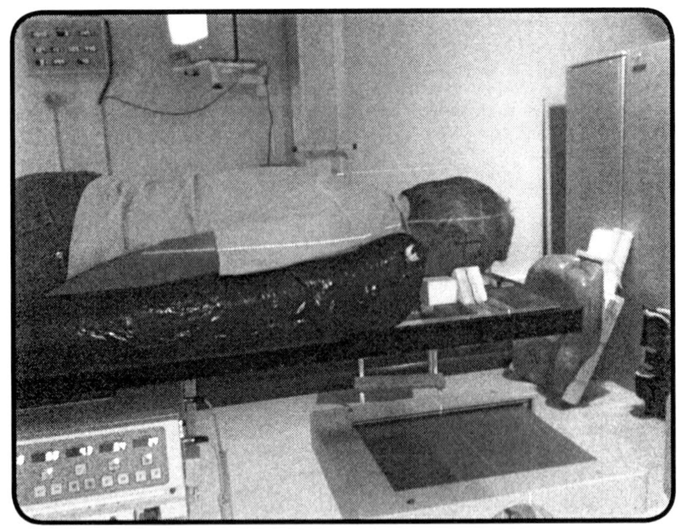

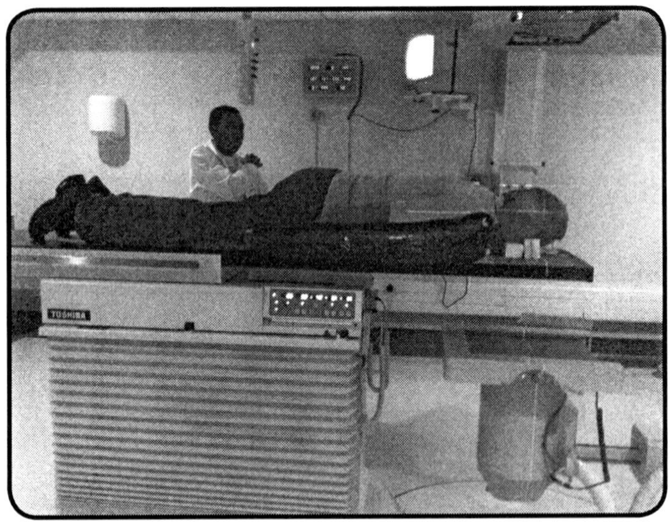

Planning for radiation (face down in the mask)

We arrived home seven hours after leaving this morning, and I was totally exhausted. I had a cup of tea and then went to lie down for half an hour, but couldn't get comfortable. My other hip has been giving me a bit of trouble over the last couple of days, so between that and the chest, I gave up and climbed into a nice hot bath instead. I'm feeling much better now. This is surreal. Craig is the one who needs attention. I can't help feeling that the forces of evil are ganging up against us.

We're eating leftovers for supper and planning an early night. I'm having breakfast with my dear friend Edith tomorrow morning. Her daughter, Lisa, has major health problems, too. She was diagnosed with cervical cancer, and only after her womb was removed did the doctors discover that the cancer had in fact spread to her womb. She underwent chemotherapy and a course of radiation therapy, and for the next two years she appeared to be normal, but now she has taken a serious downward turn. I decided that Edith and I deserve a hearty chinwag.

Monday, 19 April 2010

As suspected, the planning procedure has to be repeated, so we'll be going there again tomorrow. I wonder how many hours we've spent in The Hospital. Things are getting so complicated that I never know what they're going to do next. Some days I feel as though I cannot carry on because there are so many hurdles to cross. I've prayed a lot for Craig, because he's not doing well, and a daily chat to God keeps my batteries charged. I've got to keep my hopes up. Writing this down is a way of speaking to myself, urging myself to keep going. So many times I've wished I could take the pain and anxiety away from this man. To watch what he's going through is the toughest thing I've ever had to do.

I recall when my daughter, Debbie, was a little girl. I would sit in waiting rooms outside medical theatres whilst doctors performed plastic surgery on her hands and bone surgery on her leg, sometimes at the same time, under the same anaesthetic. On one occasion, she came out of theatre bandaged from arms to feet. The only visible part of her body was her head, except for which she resembled an Egyptian mummy. Now, many years later, I again find myself outside operating theatres, anxiously waiting for my son to emerge, with his head bandaged. Oh how

I wish I could make this tragedy disappear! I spend hours trying to imagine how Craig feels, physically and mentally. What a burden he's been given, what an abysmal burden, but still, he never complains. He's been known to scream in pain when the headaches are bad, but he rarely talks about it. He cried all the way to the hospital once, holding his head in his hands because of the pain. I was driving the car in the usual heavy traffic, and his distress was mortifying.

Wednesday, 21 April 2010

I'm so, so tired, having had three full days at the hospital, but at last the radiation has begun. From now on our visits will be shorter. Setting up the mapping and planning the radiation was very involved, and they had to get it spot on, which they have now done. The first ten-minute session happened today. We're all taking one day at a time. Craig is scheduled to have thirty treatments. Presently I'm taking him, but he seems to think he can go it alone next week. I'm not listening to him, but we shall see. He's concerned about all the petrol I'm using to run back and forth, and he feels that if he drives himself, he can drop Georgie at the shop in the mornings and go straight back there afterwards. He worries a lot about the shop.

Once again I left the house at 6:00 a.m. yesterday and today, and got home after 3:00 pm. I probably sound repetitive when I talk about the hours spent in that hospital, but I've never talked about the same episode more than once. It happens again and again and again.

The oncology division is very proficient. Craig was fine after the treatment today, but he phoned a moment ago to say he thinks he's now got the flu. What next? The oncology section is very cold, because they have to keep the machines cool, and he can't wear a jacket for the treatment, so I hope he's okay.

There are some eye-openers in that section of the hospital. One of the familiar faces we've seen is a short, balding man, who scurries about from one room to another. We've been told he's a professor. He's *the* professor, and of course they call him Prof. He's as casual as can be, but everyone respects him. What I admire about him is that even though he's the big boss in radiation oncology, he's never too busy to stop and talk to a patient, or to lend a hand to a nurse pushing a trolley. Yesterday he was passing by our group of "patient patients", waiting for whatever we were waiting for. There was a mother and child, a little girl of about seven, whose head was completely bald, no doubt from chemotherapy. They'd been there longer than we had and all the time the little girl had a broad smile on her face, as though the world was her oyster. Spotting the child, the Prof stopped.

"Hello, angel," he said kindly, "and how's my girl today?" His hand rested on her head and her grin grew even wider.

"I'm very fine, Prof," she said, "and how are you?"

"All the better for seeing you, Lindiwe. Is your treatment finished yet?"

Lindiwe carried on grinning. "One more to go, and then my Mommy says my hair will grow again."

The mother forced a tired smile. Her eyes said it all; and as the Prof walked past her, he leaned over to give her hand a gentle squeeze. I wondered how many more birthdays that little girl would have.

Two little boys were playing on the floor. They were obviously twins, but one was tubby, and the other was painfully thin. Seeing children in that state is horrendous, but they tend to develop extraordinary strength and determination. This has been such an experience for me, sitting on the outside looking in. There are many diverse types of people there, different colours and cultures, men, women, and children. They have differing types and levels of cancer. Some are on crutches, some are thin, some have hair, and some don't. But they all have one thing in common—the desire to get back the life they once had. I'm humbled, as I sit there amongst positive, smiling cancer patients, who inspire one another in love and hope. When Craig arrived, as a new kid on the block, they talked him through the process of radiation therapy, explaining possible side effects, but nevertheless allaying any fears he may have had. I wonder how many of them will make it. I wonder if my own son will make it, but I don't often think of that. I've chosen to believe he will.

The place itself is spotless; even the toilets are clean. One gets the feeling of being in a posh private infirmary, a massive contrast to the pandemonium of the rest of the hospital. The staff in radiation oncology are amazing, and throughout the recent trauma, we've been enormously encouraged by their diligence. They deal with vast numbers of patients daily, but they treat everyone with kindness and respect.

Sunday, 25 April 2010

Craig's so-called "flu" turned out to be a false alarm, and his health is good. After three radiation treatments, I can see that this is going to be a long haul, but fortunately the waiting is shorter in this department. There are never more than three or four people in front of him, and each patient has ten minutes in the radiation room, so the most we would wait is an hour; but on Friday we waited only five minutes.

The drive to the city in the mornings takes up to one and a half hours in peak hour traffic. Vehicles are often backed up for miles. For me, Gillooly's Interchange is a nail-biting part of the trip, where I have to move from the far left lane to the right hand side of a five-lane motorway, so I now consider myself South Africa's best woman driver. Gillooly's is purported to be the biggest interchange in the southern hemisphere. On one rush hour journey, Craig had a violent headache and kept insisting that he needed a cigarette to lessen the pain. He lit up, shaking as he did so, and the inevitable happened. As I was negotiating Gillooly's, he dropped the cigarette and couldn't find it. Panic stations ensued. There was nothing I could do but pray the cigarette wouldn't burn a massive hole in the carpet. The combination of Craig's aching head and partial blindness, and my stressful driving campaign, did not augur well, but he did manage to put his hand on the cigarette, and no damage was done. It was just another day in the life of the Edwards family.

On Friday we were in the hospital for a total of twenty minutes, then back in the car, but it took only forty-five minutes to get home because the traffic had calmed down. I dropped Craig at his house, turned around, and drove back to work, about twenty-five kilometres from where he lives. By the time I got into my office it was 10:00 a.m., and I had been driving for four hours, except for the twenty minutes in the clinic! How's that for a trip! I work for my eldest son Doug, who has said I can come into the office if and when I am able, and not to stress about it. Officially, I only work two days a week, but have taken time off to deal with Craig. Radiation is scheduled to take place from Mondays to Fridays, with weekends off, so I'll be doing the necessary transporting, because Ian works a six-day week.

Thus far the radiation has not had any side effects, but the headaches are worse than they have ever been. Once a week, after his treatment, Craig will be seeing a radiation oncologist. He's been issued medication, which hopefully will kick in soon, thus reducing the pressure on his brain. There'll be no radiation today because it's Sunday. I phoned him this morning, and he was in the shop with Georgie. He's inclined to stress about what's going on there without him. Tomorrow we'll be off to the hospital again, and this goes on for another six weeks or so.

Saturday, 1 May 2010

I wonder if it's only this family who runs into drama in The Hospital? It even occurs in radiation oncology, although in this instance it was through no fault of theirs. Craig was the only patient in the waiting room. When the radiographer appeared to call him in for his treatment, he asked if I'd like to come and watch.

"Oh yes," I said, "But I thought no one was allowed in there."

"You can watch us set him up," I was told, "then after that you can sit in our office and view the procedure on the television screen."

"Thank you," I said, feeling very privileged.

We walked through a metal gate down a short passage that led to the radiation room. It was exactly the same as the planning room, with huge machines set up around the radiation table. The body cast and mask were lying in wait. Craig climbed onto the table and lay face down in the mask, which was fixed to the table so his head could not move. The radiographer explained that from then on he was not allowed to move for the duration. The machines were adjusted so that the beams focused exactly over the tumour, according to the MRI scan, just as planned. Everything was now on the computer, making certain of absolute precision.

"Okay," the radiographer said, "all set. Now, once I press the timer, we must get out of here. Okay?"

"Okay," I said nervously.

He smiled. "The radiation takes only a few minutes," he assured me. "You can come and watch the live movie now."

He pressed the button, or flipped the switch, or whatever he had to do, and made his way to the door, with me hot on his tail. Having shut the door behind him, we marched down the passage and through the gate, which locked electronically behind him. That was the first time I realised how potent radiation really is. We couldn't be exposed to it, but Craig was under its penetrating power. Then the big oops came! The lights went out in a typical South African power cut. I gasped, petrified. My son was in the middle of radiation treatment.

The radiographer took my arm. "Don't worry," he said gently, "We have emergency generators. I'll have to go find the technician. You go into the office. You can keep an eye on him on the screen."

A lady radiographer was in the office. She offered me a seat.

"He'll be fine," she assured me, "He'll just have to lie there a bit longer than usual."

"Will he know what's happened?" I asked.

"Not yet, but I'm going in there, so I'll tell him."

"Can you get through the gate?"

She grinned. "There's a Plan B for everything," she assured me.

Keeping my eyes glued to the screen, I watched her enter the room and make a few adjustments to the machines. Craig never moved an inch. I'd never seen anyone so rigid in my life. Poor fellow appeared to have solidified. It seemed to take ages for them to solve the problem, but they did get everything working again, and the treatment was successful. When he came out, his face was squashed and red, but he was none the worse for wear. He figured he'd done better than the British Grenadiers standing to attention outside Buckingham Palace!

And so the season progresses. I wonder what sort of a winter we're in for, but we won't get the warm clothes out just yet.

Chapter 11

Seven weeks of radiation therapy was completed, with no side effects whatsoever. I drove Craig there each day for the first two weeks, but he'd made up his mind to go it alone, which Mother Hen here wasn't too happy about in the beginning. But he managed exceedingly well and drove himself back to his shop in Alberton afterwards on a daily basis. Often I would look after the shop while he was having his treatment. I was overawed by the customers who would come in and tell me what a marvellous son I had. Everyone was rooting for him. Some of his regular customers would even come into the shop for no other reason than to find out how he was doing. He used to refill customers' ink cartridges, and when he wasn't there, they were happy to leave the cartridges and collect them later. If they wanted new products, they would help me to identify them on the shelves. They supported his business, but more than that, they supported him in his personal struggle.

That boy has made me so very proud. Over the past two years he has adjusted his vision to accommodate every area of his life. Although he has no peripheral vision on the right side, he turns his head, whereas we would shift our eyes. He says he doesn't see like we do, but it doesn't stop him from doing most things. I nearly fell over backwards when the driver's licensing department recently renewed his licence. I've heard they take bribes, but I'm sure Craig didn't go that route—he's not wealthy enough! I pulled his leg about bribery, only to be informed that his driving is a whole lot better than mine. I disagree, but that has nothing to do with his eyesight!

Tuesday, 27 July 2010

Last month Ian and I celebrated our fortieth wedding anniversary. We had a scrumptious dinner at Doug and Lindy's house with all the boys and their spouses. Once again, we missed Debbie, but I know that one of these days we'll have a proper family reunion with all our kids.

Last week Craig went for his first check-up, six weeks after completion of the radiation. The oncologist was happy with the way he was handling things. Check-ups in oncology are much easier than check-ups in neurosurgery. One doesn't have to wait *quite* so long, and the waiting room isn't *quite* so crowded, but the unfinished crocheted blanket still comes along for the ride. Craig could have gone on his own, but I think he secretly enjoys my company, and I'm interested to hear what the doctors have to say because he has a tendency to tell only half the story.

Craig's tumour headaches have completely gone, and he says the only headaches he gets are the normal ones we all get from stress and tiredness. He lost most of his hair from the radiation, and it's now showing signs of growing, but this is a slow process. We were told that the radiation continues to do its work for a couple of months after completion, so he wears a beanie, which is fine, because the winter isn't over yet.

Craig booked an MRI for 2 December, so we'll have to wait a few months before we know exactly what's happening inside his head. I anticipate good news.

Meanwhile, life is back to normal. We've seen two years of miracles, and I have no doubt whatsoever that there are more to come. Brian and Nicky are getting married in October, and Craig will be one of the two best men. When he was diagnosed, we didn't even know if he would see another birthday. He's faced countless stumbling blocks since he was rushed to hospital on that fateful night, but the Lord has preserved him all along.

Saturday, 21 August 2010

Edith and I enjoyed some quality time together this afternoon. Even though we come from entirely different backgrounds, we have a lot in common, such as the ability to laugh over those unspeakable details that have turned us into "older women". Today we talked about things we don't understand, pondering over why her dear mother, eighty-eight years old, and whose life was devoted to loving and caring for others, is now in an old age home with no quality of life, wondering *what* she is, rather than *who* she is, unable to fend for herself at all. I could offer no answer to Edith's dilemma, except to say that God, in His wisdom, knows all things and still has a plan and purpose for the old lady's life. I think most of us fear old age, but there's not much we can do about it.

Then of course there's her daughter, Lisa. Edith shares my heartache as she watches her child's pain. Lisa is little older than Craig and has three lovely daughters of her own. Edith and I have prayed and talked about our kids for hours, sharing our innermost feelings on their respective conditions. Edith herself was healed from critical cancer some years ago, and she knows that God could heal Lisa, too. Yet we both have questions. We will continue to pray, but only God has the answers.

I'm going through a time of realising the importance of friends in our lives. My friends have been a blessing throughout these difficult months. I think that when one travels a road such as our family has been on, priorities change, and one takes on a new perspective on life. I have a friend of almost fifty years by the name of Lorraine. She knew all my children when they were growing up, and I cherish her friendship more than ever now. My friends make up a huge part of my support system, and I'd like them to know how grateful I am for their part in helping us through our travail.

Saturday, 16 October 2010—Brian's wedding

Nicky, Brian, and Craig

The best man's speech

Brian and Nicky's wedding in October was lovely. Apart from his bald head and a mammoth scar on the back of it, Craig looked as normal as everyone else. His sense of humour prevailed during his speech, no doubt egged on by a few drinks. On the surface, he looked fine, but the trepidation was ever present. What did the future hold for him? How would it all end?

Monday, 27 December 2010

As Brian and Nicky celebrated their honeymoon with a trip to the Maldives, Doug and Lindy celebrated twenty years of their marriage with a trip to Zanzibar— all that in October. And already we've seen another Christmas come and go. That's what I wrote in my journal today. I talked about having lived through sixty-seven Christmases. Phew! There's a reason to take a deep breath and count my blessings! I have so much still to do, and as I get older, there seems to be a lot more to cram into one year. I suppose it's because we once had all the time in the world and now we don't. There's the thing—we *think* we have all the time in the world, but in fact we know not what lies around the next corner, and we should never take our destiny for granted. Treasure the present, I say, because the past is but a memoir and the future a stranger. One thinks a lot about such things when a loved one's life hangs in the balance. Perhaps it's time to take stock and try to right the wrongs in our lives.

It was lovely to have our three sons for Christmas, and sad that Debbie couldn't have been there, but she was surely in all of our hearts. We did the big traditional dinner thing again with friends and family, and I thanked God for another year of His favour.

Wednesday, 29 December 2010

Craig's progress over the last few months has been remarkable. Six months after his radiation treatment he had another MRI scan, which showed that residual tumour exists. He will have another check-up at the end of January.

I often wonder what goes through my son's mind on a day-to-day basis. I can imagine, but I can *only* imagine. How would I feel? I can't answer that. It's so easy for folks to say, "I know how you feel," but they don't. They can't. If they've undergone a similar experience, then perhaps they may have an inkling, but even then, it's only perhaps. As human beings, we're quick to assume how other people feel, given a certain circumstance, but we will never know exactly, even if we've been through an almost identical experience. We're all unique, we feel differently, we react differently, we even agonise differently. So I'll never know how Craig feels, even if he tells me. By no means can I fully understand his pain. I have pain too, but it's not his pain. I hurt when I look at him, when I observe his expressions, when I touch his hands. My heart aches, it burns, it grieves. But it's not his grief. He hides his pain. He hides it to save others the sorrow of his own distress. He's very unselfish; he always has been. As a mother, I wish I could take some of his pain upon myself; I wish I could take all of it, but this is the cross he has to bear, and I can't do anything about it. All I can do is love him and pray for him; and that I will do until one of us departs from this earth.

Chapter 12

January 2011

In July of this year my mother, who lives near Melbourne, Australia, with my two younger sisters, will be turning ninety. My brother Tony and I have been blessed with tickets to Australia for her celebration, so started making plans, but to be so far from home frightened me a little. The consensus was that I should make the trip and let go of my middle son for a while. My spirit told me we should go in April instead of July. Tony thought that was a daft idea, so I used the weather, school holidays, and so forth as excuses. For some reason I wasn't happy about going in July. The more I thought about it, the more I felt that April was a better time to go.

Tony succumbed after we decided to ask Mother what she would prefer. Her reaction was "the sooner the better", so the flights are booked, and I have plans to spend Easter, the last few days of my holiday, in Perth with my dear friend Yvonne. This lady has been one of my strongest sources of encouragement. She's had an amazing knack of cropping up in emails when I'm feeling downhearted, bringing forth encouragement and inspirational scriptures from God's Word.

We can get so caught up in a particular situation that we overlook the life that continues to take place around us.

Periodically I have to remind myself that I have other kids to pray for, and other things to do. There's my son, Doug, for instance, who's about to go sailing round the world on a yacht. Well, maybe not around the *whole* world, but it's certainly a grand adventure, or so I'm told. An opportunity of a lifetime, I hear, but he's not going for a leisure trip, no siree; he's going to learn to become a sailor! Hmm—some folks have the urge to jump out of aeroplanes, some to hunt for lions, and others to test the high seas. He'll be flying to Malaysia, and sailing up the coast of Malaysia and Thailand, en route to the southern Maldives, with a friend who owns the yacht and a couple of gents in their sixties and seventies, one of whom was a mariner in his younger days, and the other who has some sailing experience, but not at sea. The owner is a hardened sailor, but Doug has no experience at all. These four gentlemen make up the crew. The idea is to get the boat back to the Seychelles, where it belongs, but Doug will only be going part of the way, because he has a business back home to run. Do what you will, my boy, and I hope you have a good time! A month away from land is an interesting quest indeed.

Tuesday, 8 February 2011

Things are not looking good. I don't know how else to describe it. Long story short, we went to get the results of the last MRI. Craig has been fairly well for the past few months, but over the last couple of weeks, he has felt all the old symptoms. A radiation oncologist explained that the tumour is rampant, describing it as "significant disease". Craig will never again be able to have radiation because what he has had is enough for life, and any more would destroy him. He's been referred back to the neurosurgeons (scheduled to meet on Friday, 17 February), and they will decide whether or not they can operate again. The drawback is that after two major operations and seven weeks of intense radiation, they have not been able to eradicate the tumour, and they don't seem to think they ever will.

We will hold on to every last bit of hope, and I will go with him again next week, but the medical prognosis is discouraging. As usual, Ian is pragmatic about the situation. He's fully aware of the gravity of Craig's condition, but he waits for results, rather than making assumptions. I, on the other hand, take refuge in talking about it, and Ian often feels that I'm upsetting myself by so doing. At times I've felt that he's a bit insensitive, but that's his way of dealing with it. This has been grim for all of us, and because we have different coping mechanisms, it can be trying on relationships. I've seen families get into confrontation when they should be pulling together in a crisis. Our family is no different. Strong words have been spoken when one person feels that another is behaving irrationally. We deal with our feelings differently, and because of this, misunderstanding can arise. But fortunately, whatever altercations we've had have been quickly resolved. A life is at stake, and I don't think any of us have lost sight of that.

Yesterday was another long day, and when we got the news of how bad the tumour is, I was closer than I have ever been to breaking down in front of my boy, but I managed to hold it together and fought back the tears until I got home. Even then, I didn't cry for long. I'm aware that it's okay to do that sometimes, but I feel the need to be strong, because I know in my heart how Craig relies on me. Again we waited five hours in the pharmacy for the medication. While sitting there I made a decision that never again would I remonstrate about the long waits in that hospital. I choose to see the time as an opportunity to enjoy five more quality hours with my son. He was getting a bit frustrated with the wait because he wasn't feeling well, so I turned to him and said, "Hey, think of this as a bonus. You get to spend five extra hours with your Mommy!"

He thought for a moment, a little grin on his face, and then chirped, "The only problem is my Mommy didn't give me anything to spend!" Continuing with his humour, he made one of his usual remarks about my knitting.

"Crocheting," I said.

"Whatever. What is it anyway?"

"A blanket."

"Who for?"

"I'm taking it to Australia," I replied, "for your cousin Colette."

"So when am I getting one?"

"Aha," I chuckled, "So now my crocheting's getting useful, eh?"

"Maybe."

"Okay," I said, "Here's the deal. When I get back I'll make you one, but you have to promise you won't whinge about the movement of the seats while I work on it."

Sigh. "Okay. How long will it take?"

"Normally about a year," I told him, "But with all the hours we spend in this place, it'll be finished in no time!"

"Will it have all those colours?"

"Uh-huh."

Notwithstanding the debacles in that hospital, I commend the people highly for what they've done for our son. What a privilege to have been allowed to sit by his side through it all. I can safely say that no other doctors could have done more for him. Yes, the biopsy results were lost, and yes, mistakes were made, but the doctors themselves have been exceptional.

I realise I may have to cancel my Australian trip because of the current state of affairs, but I believe I am meant to somehow see my mother. Then there's the question of my lungs. I'm almost at the end of my tether with that disaster. Having been coughing for almost a year, I've now been issued a cortisone pump. But it doesn't help, so I'm getting agitated. My late father used to say, "These things are sent to try us". My question is, "For how long?"

The good news comes in the form of the knowledge that God has graced us with a son called Craig, who, like most children, has caused us some upsets during his life, but who today we feel honoured to have raised. If I had to do it all again, I would have no hesitation, from the day before my birthday, almost forty years ago, when I gave birth to him, throughout the course of his childhood, amidst the heartache of failure and the joy of success, to the pain of his illness, and the ultimate vision of memories that will live in my heart forever. I remind myself of these things on a regular basis, because I have no idea where this road is leading. All my children are a blessing and I will never lose sight of that.

Saturday, 19 February 2011

The scheduled appointment on Friday the eighteenth at the neuro clinic, fifth floor, Green Block, turned into yet another nightmare. Nothing in that establishment comes to pass without a foregoing nightmare. As usual, we waited hours in the neuro clinic to see a surgeon, following all the standard procedures, before actually gaining access to his consulting room. First the patient has to stand in a queue to hand in his Blue Book. Every registered patient has to have one, a small book with appointments and other relevant information. After handing that in at the counter, you try to find a seat, where you wait indefinitely. Then, with the use of a loudspeaker, they call out names, and with a bit of luck your name is amongst them, at which point you join the queue to pay for your visit, according to your income, which has been recorded by a code. Once that's done, you return to your seat for a longer indefinite period.

The doctors don't normally arrive until after 9:00 a.m. or 10:00 a.m., because they've been doing their rounds in the wards. You've been there since about 7:00 a.m., due to the crowds. Now you've got plenty of time to chat, or in Craig's case, to go out and take a smoke break. He wouldn't be able to do that if I weren't holding the fort for him. There's a strong chance they'll call his name whilst he's not there, in which case I'd be on the cell phone to him very sharply!

When the doctors arrive, names are called out, but this time there's no loudspeaker, so the sister with the very loud voice stands at the top of the room, exercising her lungs copiously. All the names in the lucky draw go up to collect their pink files. This is a patient's personal file, which is often empty, because the chances are that the past information has been lost. If you didn't get there early, your name won't be in the first batch.

Next you move into a line of chairs outside the doctors' consultation rooms, and as a doctor becomes available, you shuffle along the line, till you eventually get your appointment with one of the doctors.

When we entered the consulting room that day, the surgeon studied the MRI scans, read the oncologist's report, and promptly gave Craig what I now term "the death sentence". We've always been aware that this tumour is life-threatening, but thus far no one has actually told him he's going to die. This doctor said it as he deemed it to be. He wasn't heartless, but he was frank. He was a young man, most likely still an intern, though I'm not sure of that.

"Craig," he said, looking directly at me, "This is not good news."

"It never is," Craig said, "But it's how you look at it, isn't it?"

The doctor looked surprised at Craig's approach. He was studying the file in front of him, which in this case, did have something in it.

"You've had this thing for a long time," he said, "This is very unusual."

"I know," Craig replied, smiling. "I'm an unusual person."

"Do you understand this tumour? Have you read it up on the Internet?"

"No," Craig replied, "I don't need to. I know what it's doing inside my head and that's quite enough for me. I'm the one who can feel it."

The doctor looked at me.

"I've checked it out," I told him.

"So you know the life expectancy?"

"Yes."

"Right. Then let me explain. Every time we operate, the risk of damage to the brain becomes greater."

"What are the risks?" I asked.

"This tumour is out of control. It's going into areas it hadn't invaded before. It's not entirely clear on the scans. We can tell only if we open Craig up."

"Then do it," said my unyielding son, "I want this thing outa here!"

The doctor sighed. "It's not that simple. We could easily damage something. This monster is going bananas in there. You could say we're dealing with the unknown."

"This is a teaching hospital," Craig said, "You could learn from it."

The young surgeon grinned. I don't think he'd come across a Craig-type patient before. He looked at me again, as though seeking some sort of approval.

Reluctantly, I smiled. "He wants you to operate," I said.

"Is that so, Craig?"

"Mother is always right," came the reply.

"Okay," said the surgeon, "But I have to warn you of the dangers."

"I thought you already did?"

"No. It gets worse. There are two choices. Neither of them is good." When no one said anything, he continued, "If you do not have this surgery, you probably have two or three months to live. If you do have it, it might give you an extra two or three months."

"I see," said Craig. "Then I'll go for option two."

"I'm not finished," the surgeon added.

I didn't want to hear this. I wanted to get the hell out of there and run for my life. But we weren't talking about my life. We weren't even talking about my son's life. We were talking about his death. My thoughts began to scream, "Wake me up, wake me up! This is the worst nightmare I've ever had! You have to wake me up!"

The surgeon's X-ray eyes penetrated my head.

"You did know about this tumour ma'am? You said you read about it."

"Yes."

"Then you know . . ."

"Yes."

"I'm really sorry," he said and when no one said anything again, he continued.

"If you have the surgery, there are two possibilities, fifty-fifty, I'd say. One, you could be reasonably well for the last few months of your life, and two, you could be severely damaged." He didn't wait for us to ask how. "You could be totally blind . . ."

"I can deal with that," Craig said.

"Or, you could be partially paralysed down the left side, as in a stroke. Or you could have brain damage and not be able to speak. Or you could be retarded. Do you hear what I'm saying?"

"I want the operation," Craig emphasised.

"Okay," said the young surgeon. "Go up to the neuro ward right now. I heard there's a vacant bed."

"Unbelievable!" I exclaimed.

"No, I can't do that," Craig argued, "I have to go home first. I don't have my stuff. I need time to prepare."

I explained to him in one short sentence, that if he didn't go now he'd lose the bed.

"You obviously know this place," the surgeon said.

"That I do. Come Craig, I'll ask Dad to collect your clothes from your house and bring them here later."

The surgeon told us we'd have to check in at admissions first, and then Craig would need to have the preparatory tests which had to be done before surgery. We thanked him and left him to deal with the umpteen dozen patients who were waiting outside his door.

After walking down to Yellow Block on the same floor, we waited for two hours to get the relevant paperwork completed. I hate that place. There's one particularly sour-faced woman whom you have to get past before you can do anything else. She doesn't tell you to sit down and wait; she merely grabs your request for admission form and rudely points you towards the seating. If you dare to ask a question, you'd think by the expression on her face that she's going to shout, "Off with her head!" You can be certain you'll be put to the back of the queue, if you're not put to death.

At last they called Craig's name, and after yet another slow procedure of filling out forms, he got his stamp of approval to proceed to the ward. But first the various tests had to be done, and we walked backwards and forwards in that colossal building, talking in a more melancholy fashion than usual. I saw in Craig a mature and sensible man who spoke about how he was going to provide for Georgie's welfare, and how fortunate he was for being given the time to prepare. He spoke about his future in Heaven, and how he would get to find out what it was really like.

"Mother," he said, "What is your perception of Heaven?"

I was staggered. "You know what it is."

"So tell me again," he smiled, but he didn't give me a chance to reply. "This is great. I'm gonna get there before you do!"

"Craig!"

"What?"

"Don't talk like that!"

"Don't you envy me? I've got an express ticket . . ."

I couldn't handle this. "Shut up!" I exclaimed, "Stop it, Craig! I can't deal with this!"

"I'm sorry, Ma," he said gently, "I didn't mean to upset you."

I touched his arm, knowing this was his way of dealing with the terrible news he'd received.

"It's okay," I told him, "but please don't joke about it. It's burning me up."

He didn't look at me when he said, "You mustn't be upset, Mother. We all have to die, you know."

"Yes," I said, fighting back the tears, "But your kids aren't supposed to go before you do."

He didn't reply, and I wished I hadn't said that, because I knew that he'd be more upset about us than he was about himself. I'd have to try and assure him that we'd be fine, even if I didn't believe it. *Oh God,* I thought, *can't you just take all of this away? Can't we be the same as we were before? Can't we have our former lives back? I'll do anything, anything, to have my boy the way he was before this horrible monstrosity took over!* God didn't answer.

Despite this heart-rending conversation, I felt a speck of joy in my spirit, because my son didn't seem afraid and was able to share his feelings with me. I told him that God had a plan for his life, whether it was long or short. He has often been a little closed to listening to me talk about spiritual things; but he was open to anything yesterday, apparently not out of fear, but of contentment. Since he was now going to be stuck in a hospital ward, he asked me to arrange for his legal aid to visit him with a view to transferring the shop into Georgie's name. He was determined to get what was left of his life into order. Once again we walked the whole length of the fifth floor, with a number of detours via elevators and stairs for blood tests and chest X-rays, eventually ending up on the sixth floor, in Blue Block. Through the familiar metal-rimmed doors we went, observing with a head shake, the dent that Craig's bed had made after his first operation.

The nurses gathered round with a unanimous, "Welcome back, Mr Craig. But where are you going to sleep? There are no beds here!"

Ay, yi yi, yi yi ! You are convinced it won't happen again, but it does!

"But the doctor said . . ."

The senior nurse shrugged her shoulders. "There have been many motor accident patients and of course when they come in, they automatically get the beds. When that doctor's finished consulting, I'll call him up here to show him he doesn't know what he's talking about. You can wait."

So what's another wait? We'd been waiting forever anyway.

"You see," said my loving son, "We should have gone home."

"Nope," I emphasised.

"You're gonna catch the five o'clock traffic . . ."

"I don't care."

What I failed to mention here is that my left hip had been giving me trouble for some time. I've known I'd need another hip replacement, but "me, myself, and I" has not been my priority, so I'd been putting up with it. However, on this day I had decided to bring my crutch, and thank goodness for that, because by now we'd been at the hospital for some seven hours, and my rickety bones needed help.

A different surgeon arrived about an hour later. Seeing me on a crutch, I was convinced he thought I was the patient, because he apologised to me for the wait and said I'd soon have a bed! My loving son, of course, would have been quite happy to leave me there and go home. The surgeon marched off and somehow "made a plan" as we would say in South Africa. So Craig, minus his overnight bag, was admitted at last.

After a hard day at work, Ian dragged himself off to collect Craig's gear from his house, and then undertook the journey to The Hospital after dinner that night. He had to get special clearance to get into the building, because there are no visiting hours in the evening. When he got back, he told me that our son looked comfortable in his bed and all was well.

Chapter 13

The tale of Doug's trip on the high seas turned into a treacherous escapade. When I heard about it on his return, I was glad that I had not been aware of what was taking place at the time. One son to fret about was enough. I jokingly enquired about pirates. When he said they had narrowly missed those, he wasn't joking. And I thought pirates existed only in storybooks. The planned trip was supposed to be half work and half play. They would moor at various places and do a bit of sightseeing, which they did manage to do, but there was a lot more work than play. After an intriguing visit to Thailand, it should have taken six days to reach the Maldives, but they ultimately anchored after eleven gruelling days and nights of storms and gale winds, which pushed them back six hundred miles into the Bay of Bengal. The wind speed was so high they had to harness themselves to the rails to avoid being washed overboard. They felt as though they were in a washing machine. One time they nearly collided with floating oil barrels and narrowly avoided other vessels when the radar system malfunctioned in heavy seas. Doug fell and cut his knee open and had to stitch himself up with a sewing needle. I know this would not have gone down well with him because he can't stand the sight of blood.

No one got any sleep for days; they were hallucinating and genuinely thought they were going to die. Everyone was praying. He said it was a terrifying experience.

Back home Lindy was worried, because there was no communication. Altogether, a bad time was had by all. The journey took five and a half weeks instead of the intended four, but Doug flew back in one piece, leaving the others to continue their exploit. Sometimes it's better when sons keep their mothers in the dark.

Monday, 28 February 2011

It's now ten days since Craig's admission to hospital. He was told by the Afrikaans neurosurgeon that his surgery was scheduled for today, but guess what? It didn't happen! We're still in the dark about everything. Someone said Craig will be informed tomorrow regarding the new arrangements, but I don't think they know what tomorrow means. We're all shattered. Craig was primed for surgery today, and so were we as a family—but now this. If someone else were relating this story to me, I would think they were joking. The whole set-up is a shambles. After admission, Craig remained in neuro ward 456 for three days and was then moved up to the ninth floor, into the renal ward, the reason being that, as is commonplace, his bed in neurosurgery was required for someone else. They shunt patients about like railway carriages. I've heard it said that to the Chinese the number "456" is symbolic of good luck! How ironic is that? Could it be that the person to whom Craig's bed was allocated was Chinese? If one looks at it that way, *somebody* got lucky!

Rarely has a doctor of any sort visited Craig, and because he's so easy-going, no one has bothered about him. The renal ward isn't full, because most of the patients are daily visitors who come in for dialysis and go home again. Craig's constant companion has been a prisoner, whose ankle is chained to the bedpost most of the time. A prison guard sits at the bottom of his bed, facing away from his assignment, because he watches

TV incessantly. For sure, there is a television set in that ward! It doesn't have an aerial, so the reception is bad, but no one is unduly concerned about that—it's better than no TV at all. Craig could easily get out of bed to sit on a chair and join in the viewing, but he maintains the prison guard watches nothing but African football, and he's not about to argue with that guy! One day the prisoner got out of bed and walked across to the nearby window, dragging the long chain behind him. When the guard jumped up, making a bee-line for him, the prisoner looked him up and down in disdain.

"D'you think I'd jump nine floors, even if I could open this window?" he protested.

The guard retreated back to his television programme, and the prisoner showed Craig the thumbs up.

I asked him what this prisoner had done to be jailed. His response was that he didn't know and he didn't want to! The prisoner's girlfriend visits daily, clad in designer clothes, sporting a plush leather handbag and outrageously high heeled shoes, not exactly befitting for a quick getaway, or the hospital environment. She bandies the latest technology mobile phone about for everyone to see. No one ventures to enquire about her source of income, but Craig mentioned (very quietly) that some men would do anything for a condescending woman! Mr Prisoner is clearly a ladies' man, and methinks it is not merely because he's good-looking. I suspect that Mr Prisoner and my son are on first name terms, which gives me rather an uncomfortable feeling.

Tuesday, 1 March 2011—Email

Here comes another tale of woe. I was turning into the office park where I work this morning, when a guy came up behind me and smashed into my car. Damage is extensive, and because it's an old car, despite being in excellent shape, the insurers want to write it off due to the fact that it will cost much more to fix than it's worth. Ian doesn't want to do that because they will pay out so little that I could never buy another car, so we'll have to pay in about twenty grand to make up the difference, and that is only if they replace the parts with second hand ones. Talk about stress. We'll have to borrow the money, but of course the most important thing right now is our son. Ian took the day off to sort out this affair, and we went to visit Craig together this afternoon. There's still no news. I made an effort to find a doctor, but to no avail, so will have to try again tomorrow. Craig is stressed about his business, so altogether the week isn't going well. I'm supposed to be seeing the lung specialist on Thursday. Added to that, I think I have a bit of whiplash from the accident, but foolishly or not, I honestly don't care.

Wednesday, 2 March 2011

I lost my sense of humour today. The lifts were out of order, so I trudged up the stairs from the fifth floor to the ninth floor to visit my son. Once again, I was greeted with the news that no doctor had visited him. This was just not acceptable, so I dragged myself back to the sixth floor neuro ward to try and get some action. The senior nurse was sitting at the computer and didn't bother to look up when I spoke to her. I told her that no one was checking on Craig and practically demanded to see a doctor. Of course I was told no one was available.

"I'll tell the doctor on duty when I see him," was all I could get out of her.

"Is that likely to be today?" I asked in the sweetest tone I could offer.

"I have no idea," was her disinterested reply.

"Sister, I know you're busy, but . . ."

"Yes I am," she snapped, and that was my cue to leave.

I hardly think my encounter with her was what caused a neurosurgeon to visit the renal ward this evening, but one did. Craig phoned to tell us that the African American neurosurgeon had arrived, apologising profusely for not seeing him. They had indeed forgotten all about him. This surgeon said the op will definitely be next week, though what day he could not promise. Although this has given Craig hope, I do confess that I'm as sceptical as ever.

Doug and Lindy are away, but Doug's co-director, Andrew, arranged for me to use a company car, which I took possession of today, so that helps a lot. I have an appointment to see the pulmonologist at The Hospital tomorrow. He has private rooms within the hospital building and is one of the teaching professors there, running his private practice there as well. Hopefully he will deliver some good news about my lungs. From there I'll go to see Craig.

Edith received appalling news today. Lisa's illness has spanned a couple of years, but now the family has been told the worst. Lisa and Craig have never met, but they are presently in the same hospital building, Lisa being in the private section on the seventh floor. They know about one another, often asking how the other is. Edith and I have passed in those passages, desperately running around, striving to solve one or another problem on our children's behalves. I have visited Lisa, and Edith has chatted to Craig, often in the canteen on his travels down there during visiting hours. And now she has to face the news we have both been dreading. My friend's little girl is dying. I'm devastated; We've been holding each other up for weeks, and this is the worst news we've had between the two of us. It's something no one wants to accept. I don't think Edith is accepting it; she has to keep on hoping. As a mother, there's a thread she can't let go of. Neither would I. Why is it that we don't know what to pray for any more?

Thursday, 10 March 2011

I've gone beyond believing that anything could ever go right in that madhouse. It's enough to put anyone's sanity to the test. For three solid weeks Craig lay in that bed with nothing to keep him occupied but a substandard television set and the radio that worked off his cell phone, knowing all the while that his awaited surgery would, at best, only prolong his life a few short months. The food was disgusting, and all he had to look forward to was two hours a day when we would visit and he could sit in the canteen with us. From my point of view, this meant travelling from Benoni in heavy peak hour traffic. Craig wasn't ill because of the medication, so had hours and hours to lie there, thinking and thinking. What was going through his head I do not fully know, but he kept on smiling and believing that he was going back to work a week after the op.

The hours, days, and weeks dragged by, until yesterday, when he decided go walkabout looking for the neurosurgeons. When the elevator arrived on the ninth floor, out stepped no less than six of them, including the boss, who said they were on their way to visit him. Up to this point, Craig hadn't seen him. What he had to say was surreal. They were now questioning the nature of the tumour. Because they'd been having issues with their pathologists, who'd been known to give incorrect diagnoses, and because Craig was looking so well, they didn't think he had a glioblastoma after all. The surgeon said that since surgery was so dangerous, they did not want to operate. And so they sent him home. He was told to come back for a check-up in two months and another MRI in six months, unless of course, he starts to feel ill again, in which case he must come back sooner, at which time they may consider operating. My big, big question is: Why did they let him lie around in the hospital for three weeks, anticipating a serious operation? Many other questions remain. I asked Craig if he had said anything to them about the trauma they had put us through, but he said it wouldn't make any difference; what is done is done, and no one is about to take responsibility. He is right; this is a third world country with no change looming.

So now he's home and says he's going back to work tomorrow. After receiving the "death sentence" he transferred most of his possessions, including his business, into Georgie's name, to make sure she was taken care of. He even said how fortunate he was to have been given time to set his affairs in place. Now it looks as though he's back to square one. Knowing Craig, I wonder how long he will continue to take the medication.

Meanwhile, I've seen the pulmonologist, who told me to throw away all my medication and go see a specialist physiotherapist who would sort out my problems. I do not know what to think of all this. I've paid one visit to this lady who is teaching me to do lung exercises. So far so good, but it's hard work and one has to be disciplined. Now here's the thing—my other hip continues to give me strife, so when I hobbled in to see the physiotherapist, I don't think she knew where to start!

Poor Edith is battling to come to grips with what's happening to Lisa. She's in a lot of pain, and things are looking really bad. I wish with all my heart that I could help my friend. Watching one's child suffer is the worst conceivable thing.

Saturday, 12 March 2011

The whole family have been urging me to go ahead with my proposed trip to Australia, and I do want to see my Mum, so I'm trying to get organised for the trip. I've been on the go for weeks. The uncertainty of Craig's illness is a tremendous thorn in my side, but I have at last started thinking about what I need to sort out before I leave, which does indicate that I'm virtually on my way. My brother Tony and I will be meeting on Tuesday next week to compare notes. We'll be stopping over in Sydney for a couple of days to do a bit of sightseeing before moving on to Melbourne to visit our mother and sisters.

Craig seems to be fine, so for the time being, we can relax. I will probably have to take my crutch to Australia; with the cough in tow, I'll be like a doddery old woman! I have been seeing the physiotherapist and doing the lung exercises, which I think are helping, but I do wonder if everything is all in my mind: the sickness, the cure, the whole package!

Chapter 14

The trip to Australia was wonderful. Tony and I spent quality time with our sisters, Karen and Jane, and we had a little tea party at the old age home for Mother's ninetieth. She was happy to have all her brood around her, almost certainly for the last time. The joviality was dampened in the last week by news from home that Craig wasn't doing well, but I still managed my stopover in Perth on the way back, and my Easter weekend with our friends Bill and Yvonne was a blessed ending to my Australian visit.

A few days after my return, I took Craig for his appointment at the neuro clinic. Clearly, he was under enormous stress. At one stage during the long wait he went out for a smoke and the lady sitting next to us turned to me in a slightly awkward manner and asked if I minded if she made a comment. I told her I didn't.

"Your son has his shoes on the wrong feet," she said.

"Really?" I responded.

"I hope you don't mind me telling you," she said, "but he must be awfully uncomfortable."

When he returned, I quietly told him. He was notably embarrassed.

"You should have told me," he said.

"I didn't notice. Don't your feet feel odd?"

His expression turned to sadness.

"I've got far more important things to think about," he sighed, "so no, my feet don't feel odd. Only my head does."

For the gazillionth time, my thoughts were screaming, "My son, my son," but my mouth did not speak.

That day Craig told the neurosurgeon that he could not continue under the current circumstances. The pressure in his head was intolerable, the headaches were intense, and other irregular symptoms occurred from time to time. Added to that, his vision had deteriorated again. He told the doctor he wanted to go ahead and have the operation, and once again he was informed of the serious risks involved. He was certainly under the impression that this operation would extend his life for a few more months. The surgeon agreed to admit him the following week, on the sixteenth of May, warning him yet again that he could wait up to two weeks for surgery.

As had become our habit on hospital visits, we spent time in the canteen. Craig placed his unchanging order of a Russian (sausage) and chips with coffee, and I had my Danish apple tart with tea. At such times we would chat, make calls to update the family, and ponder the possibilities that lay ahead. That day he made a resolution.

"Mom," he said in a well-known tone of voice.

"What is it Craig?"

"This is going to be my last operation."

"How do you know that?" I asked, for want of a better response.

"Oh I know," he affirmed, "because I will not be having another one."

"You mean you don't want another op?"

He sighed. "I can't go on living like this anymore, Ma. If they can't fix me this time . . ."

"Shhhh," I whispered, "I believe they are going to fix you, but don't decide that now, my boy. You may change your mind."

"No I won't," he determined. "This is the last one."

"Okay," I said ruefully, although I don't know why, because I didn't want him to have any more operations either.

"Ma," he said, "thanks for all the times you've brought me here. Thanks for all your time."

I didn't like the finality of that remark, but I told him it was my pleasure and changed the subject.

In the meantime we heard that Seve Ballesteros had taken a turn for the worse and died on the seventh of May. Over a two-year period, he had undergone four courses of chemotherapy, but lived for less than three years after contracting the tumour. It was obvious that this news disturbed Craig, because Seve's tumour was detected at around the same time as his. Seve didn't have a GBM, but he died anyway. What, I asked, was going through Craig's mind? He never talked about his fears, although I'm sure he must have had them.

Monday, 16 May 2011

Today was another downright catastrophe at the hospital. When one lives through an experience like this, one leans towards using pessimistic words, and even to thinking the worst thoughts. I think this is natural, but I also believe that we should do our best to wipe out the negativity and focus on positive things. Right now I'm struggling to find something positive to think about. In truth, I'm not thinking much at all. I'm so tired. I could happily doze off in this chair, after hours and hours at The Hospital, with countless shenanigans.

To begin with, we sat waiting in admissions. Once that was sorted out, we went up to the ward, only to be told—you guessed it—there were no beds! The sister suggested we wait for the surgeon on duty to come to the ward. She didn't know when that would be, so we sat down like a couple of street urchins and waited. We were back in the recurring dream. It was 1:00 p.m. As we waited, no less than four more potential patients arrived to get their promised beds. Five patients and no beds—how typical! The surgeon turned up at 4:00 p.m. He was the same surgeon who had admitted Craig in February for the operation that didn't take place. He informed us there'd been a disaster—another one. Patients from another large hospital had been transferred to The Hospital because their life support system had broken down—or some such story. They'd taken all our beds. One by one, the other four would-be patients left, but Craig and I continued to sit.

"We have the admission forms," I told the surgeon. "This man has come to stay."

The surgeon couldn't help grinning. "You don't give up," he said. "I'll see what I can do."

Forty minutes ticked by as he tried to get a patient from that ward transferred to another hospital so Craig could have the bed, to no avail. He chatted to us, and from what he said, we concluded that the state hospital situation in this country is much worse than even I imagined. The doctor had no solution to the problem. He tried every ward in the hospital—all full. He tried to move a patient to another hospital. He even tried to discharge a patient who wasn't ready to be discharged. Eventually, at 6:00 p.m., he told us to go home and come back in the morning. I told him he must be joking, but he said that since Craig had already been "admitted", the hospital was now responsible for his whereabouts, so therefore we could go home and they would have to admit him in the morning. Otherwise somebody would be in serious trouble for permitting an already-admitted patient out of the building without discharge papers. I'd never heard anything like that in my life.

The saga continues. Craig was warned that once he gets a bed he could wait up to *three months* before they do the op. That was unbelievable; especially when one considers that he'd been given less than three months to live if he didn't have the operation. We were told that right now they are operating only on patients who have had near fatal seizures. After a massive seizure over two years ago, Craig wasn't expected to live through the night, yet he was sent home, and surgery took place a whole month later. Now they are saying that these seizure patients will be given emergency operations and everyone else will have to wait, including the critical patients like Craig. The horror is, there are hundreds awaiting surgery, and from what I've been given to understand, everyone is being told that someone else is more important than they are.

Wednesday, 18 May 2011—Email

Craig is in hospital. After a few calls yesterday, they phoned me at 1:00 p.m. to say they had a bed, so I dashed off to pick him up and got him there shortly before 3:00 p.m. Fortunately, my own doctor's appointment was in the morning, so it worked out well, but by the end of the day I was utterly exhausted. Thank goodness we didn't have to go through admissions again.

My poor son; I left him there, knowing what a fearful time he has ahead of him. There's nothing to do there, no TV, nothing. The radio on his cell phone is once again his only consolation. He can't even read because his sight is significantly bad now. The neuro ward is awful. Most of the patients have had brain surgery, and some are brain damaged. We can only hope that he gets his op quickly. The country is falling apart. People are dying unnecessarily, and nothing is being done about it.

My chest is okay. I've been told I will live with this disease for life and will have to manage it. I've had a few trying days, but I'm seeing the pulmonologist and doing physiotherapy lung exercises daily. The doctor says I'm doing well. He maintains that stress won't affect my condition, but I disagree. I'm still walking with a crutch, no doubt until I get this second hip done, but I can't see that happening for some time, so I just get on with what I have to do.

Tuesday, 24 May 2011—Email

Another bombshell has hit us! Late on Sunday night Craig phoned to say he was having the op on Monday (yesterday). Having been moved to a different ward in the afternoon, they moved him back to the neuro ward, and early in the morning they started prepping him for the op. He had the chest X-rays, blood tests, and so forth, and they connected him up to a drip for the operation. They told him he was first into the theatre, but when that didn't happen, he waited patiently, as he is in the habit of doing. Needless to say there was no breakfast or anything to drink. I kept on phoning for news, but as they day wore on, there was none. At about 3:00 p.m. they came and told him that the operation had been cancelled.

Oh woe is me! After all we have come to know and expect in that hospital, this was a new one! Twenty-four hours later, at 3:00 p.m. today, Ian and I were there to visit him. He was still connected to the drip, but decided he'd had enough of the ward for the day and made his way down to the canteen with us. He was craving a cigarette, and fortunately for him there's an outside part of the canteen where smoking is permitted. Endeavouring to get him to quit is no longer a part of my curriculum. He once told one of the nurses in the ward that if she looked at his chart, she would see that smoking was not what was going to kill him. After that, she allowed him to leave the ward whenever he wished to go and smoke.

Yesterday afternoon they brought him food, which definitely meant there would be no surgery that day. I have to say, he was rather annoyed. This morning he saw the doctor who admitted him to the hospital and who told him that he is the one who will be doing the operation. Evidently he operated on another patient yesterday, (even though Craig had been told he was first on the list!) and that op took much longer than anticipated, so there wasn't time for any other surgery that day. Craig's op will also be a long one, so that was the end of that. He has now been told it will happen either on Thursday this week or Monday next week. He maintains that the only time you can be certain you are getting surgery is when you are anaesthetised! Even then, it wouldn't surprise me if they changed their minds again. So we wait, but at least it does not appear that he will be waiting months.

As for me, I'm washed out, but there's no quitting this mission. The on-going drive to and from the hospital each day is very tiring and nerve-racking, disagreements with taxi drivers being the order of the day. And so, my friends, that's our chapter for the day. Tomorrow we take another step and keep on climbing till we reach the top of this long ladder.

Chapter 15

Sunday, 29 May 2011

Even though this has been a heavy going ordeal for the whole family, I haven't lost sight of the fact that God is at the helm of this enormous ship. It was never going to be plain sailing, and we've all had to pull together to support Craig, but I've known all along that the definitive outcome of this voyage is in God's hands. There have been times when I've felt that He has given me just the tiniest insight into His reasons for allowing Craig's suffering, and perhaps one day I will write about those sentiments. I have, in humility, spent hours with God, praying, agonising, and even speculating about my son's well-being. I've come to realise more each day how sovereign God is. Three months ago I totally surrendered my son to Him. That may sound easy, but it was a frightfully hard thing for me to do. I might as well have been physically handing over a new-born baby to an adoptive parent, never to have any authority in that child's life again, but I knew that God is far better equipped to direct my son's journey than I could ever be. I hadn't intended to share this story within these pages, but a friend suggested that folk who may be facing a similar struggle may be inspired by my experience.

In my sun lounge, where I pray, I have an imaginary basket, which stands on the coffee table. Whenever I pray for other people, I place their names in the basket and ask God to take care of their needs. That day, I told Him that I would never again place Craig's name in the basket, because there was no longer any need to do so. I am still his mother, I still love him dearly, and I would still give my life for him if I had to, but he belongs in his entirety to the Lord, and the Lord will do His will in his life. He will direct my path and Craig's. I have prayed for guidance and wisdom for the doctors who are performing this third operation, and I thank God daily for the strength He has given Ian and me and for the son with whom He has entrusted us.

I have a CD with a beautiful song called "How Great is our God". This morning I've been listening to it and thanking God over and over again for yet another miracle He has performed in our son's life, that of enabling the surgery to take place against all odds in a state hospital. I laugh at myself when I get so amazed every time one of these miracles happens. They should be second nature to me now, because there have been so many. On a difficult voyage, with many channels to navigate, I thank the Lord for the peace that dwells within the pain.

Tuesday, 31 May 2011—Email

Craig was on the operating table for about four hours yesterday. Knowing most of the doctors is very advantageous. When Craig had his first operation, I didn't know any of them, so we didn't get any feedback. But this time I knew exactly who to look out for. As soon as I spotted a surgeon coming down the long passage, I jumped up and ran to speak to him, my faithful crutch trying hard to keep up with my leg movements. Ian and Georgie were hot on my tail. The surgeon told us that the surgery had gone extremely well, with no trauma at all, and that they had managed to remove most of the tumour, but once again, not the whole thing. He said our son was in recovery and would be out soon, which he was. When they wheeled him out, his face was a bit swollen and bloody, and the oxygen mask covered his nose, but his eyes were open and he managed a big grin as they drove him past us into the intensive care unit. Ian, Georgie, and I were calling out, "Hi Craig, we're here for you!" and we were so pleased to note that this time they did not crash him into the steel door, as they did after the first op. Tears filled my eyes and all Ian could say was, "What are you crying for? Can't you see he's okay?" *Men!* I told him to get a sex change so he could feel what I was feeling!

Whilst they were setting him up in ICU, we waited outside, whereupon and the assistant surgeon appeared. Being able to speak to two of the surgeons on the same day was more than we could have hoped for. The assistant was the young lady surgeon who had done her best to accommodate us after the second operation. In discussion with us, she explained the technicalities.

When we asked how he was doing, she said, "Oh, he's fine. After he woke up, he was telling us what to do!"

By the time we got to speak to Craig, I told him what she had said, and his reaction was, "What? I was telling the doctors what to do?"

It was quite funny. When I was talking to the lady surgeon, I couldn't stop thanking her for what they had done—and here comes another miracle: She said that all the thanks should go to God. She told me that the doctors prayed before the operation.

"As a team?" I asked, and she said no, not exactly. She prayed, and then afterwards she was talking to the chief surgeon who told her he had also prayed about the surgery. What more could I ask for than praying doctors, who acknowledge where their abilities come from? I told her I had also prayed for them, that God would give them wisdom and guide their hands that day.

"Well," she said, He certainly did that."

You know, friends—for me that acknowledgement was worth the hassles we've had in The Hospital over the past few years. We gripe about admin issues, long waits and inefficiency in certain areas, but ultimately, I think we should take stock of the good things and not focus on the problems.

We stayed with Craig for about half an hour and then left him in the doubtless capable hands of one bossy sister. He was talkative, as he generally is after surgery, wanting to know how many pipes and tubes he had, and so on. He's not in the most comfortable situation, and he wasn't looking forward to what lies ahead, but he's a strong fellow. He says he's going back to work on Thursday! He did that last time, so he's sure he can do it again. We can't stop this boy!

We'll be seeing him this afternoon and are expecting a blast because he didn't get any food last night. He had given me strict instructions about making sure they left food for him, but we were not able to get anywhere near the kitchen staff, and the supper arrived before he came out of the theatre. When I phoned last night, the sister told me he was fine, but starving, and of course there was no food to be had. He had to wait till 9:00 a.m. today to get breakfast, so had not eaten since Sunday night. Methinks Georgie and I are in big trouble! She is taking something nice for him this afternoon, but I guess that's a bit late. I think I'd better stay home this afternoon! Not likely! I'll bet he's out of ICU by the time we get there, so will be shouting for his pillow (which is in my car). We were not allowed to give it to him yesterday, and I know he's upset about that because he has categorically stated that he needs a pillow after brain surgery. I'm glad I've got his cell phone, or he'd be on it right now!

Wednesday, 1 June 2011—Email

Now listen to this: Craig was up and about today, two days after his surgery. He came out of the ward and sat in the canteen with us. This is crazy, isn't it? He told the doctor he wants to go home, and he reckons they are letting him out tomorrow (Thursday). Yesterday he was full of tubes and he says it was painful when they took them out, but today he's almost back to normal, despite the many clips in his head, which are due to come out in a couple of weeks.

There are many sad cases in The Hospital. We meet people in queues, in wards, and in clinics, and my heart cries out to them to such an extent that it pains me. Recently we met a forty-one-year-old woman called Tanya, whose eye had been destroyed by a tumour. She'd had about six operations and was now waiting to have both the tumour and her eye removed before the tumour could take hold of the other eye. She was chatting to Craig about it and I told her I would be praying for her, hoping that I'd meet up with her again to see how she was getting on. Today, we passed her and her husband in the corridor. She spotted Craig with his bandaged head and stopped to talk to him. It was like meeting an old friend! She was taken in at admissions today, but there was no bed in the ward for her, so they told her to come back tomorrow. Have we not heard this story before? She's hoping to have her operation on Monday next week. We had a big hug, and they went on their way. I'm sure I will meet her again.

Thursday, 9 June 2011

Lisa passed away yesterday. She was discharged from hospital about three weeks ago because they couldn't do any more for her. Edith was with her every day, watching her beloved daughter slowly fading away, neither eating nor drinking, until she was a mere fragment of her former self. She suffered a lot of physical pain as she lingered on in an inexplicable manner, eventually dying in her mother's arms.

One may ask, "Why, why, why? Why should a mother have to watch her child suffer and die?" It's a natural question, but not one to which we will ever find an answer. God is Sovereign and only He knows. We all have questions, but I have learned to accept the outcome of what I believe to be part of God's divine purpose for our lives. In spite of that, I am not immune to the question syndrome. I'm going through a terrible struggle at the moment. I've been crying out to God, "Lord, what is this thing called cancer, that it can destroy life in such a way?" Edith and I have walked this road together, hand in hand, loving and supporting our children, praying for them, caring for them. And now her daughter has gone, but I still have my son. It doesn't seem fair. Why Lisa, and why have you spared Craig? Even as I cry out, I know that Craig's battle isn't over yet.

He's been home a week already and is having the thirty-five clips taken out of his head tomorrow. He's still getting headaches, and his sight isn't good, but I guess that's part of the recovery process. He pulled through quicker last time, but they did say the ops get more complicated each time. Now we'll have to tell him about Lisa.

Monday, 27 June 2011

My heart ached for Edith at her daughter's funeral. No parent should have to go through that. It makes so many things about life seem meaningless.

Craig handled the news of Lisa's passing quietly, once again alone with his thoughts. I have no doubt his heart was troubled, but there was nothing anyone could have said or done to make his burden lighter. Lisa had died of cancer. Craig has cancer too.

He had his clips removed a couple of weeks ago, which made him more comfortable, and the headaches are not nearly so bad; in fact, they are presently not bad at all. However, his eyesight is worse than it has ever been, and he can't work on the computer. Georgie is still running the shop, but things are not going well. Craig can't go into the shop because he can't even see to sweep the floor, so he stays home all day, attempting to watch a blurry TV. I visit him at least twice a week, spending a couple of hours with him each time. I habitually stop at McDonald's or some such place to get him a cheese burger with chips and a soft scoop ice cream with a chocolate Flake Bar in it. He loves those. Watching him get stuck into that is such a pleasure for me. He's like a big kid with an even bigger lollipop. It reminds me of that song Burl Ives used to sing called "Big Rock Candy Mountain". How wonderful it would be if the world really was a place of lemonade springs and soda water fountains, without troubles or cares, and a dictionary that didn't include the word *stress*.

I hobble into Craig's house on my crutch, and his silly little dog, Bam, goes crazy barking at me. That dog hates everything and everybody except Craig, whom he loves with all his heart. Craig fumbles about, putting the kettle on for tea, but I end up making it because he can't see. My heart is breaking for him, but he diligently perseveres. I do worry about him being there on his own all day, but thus far he's been all right. He manages to get up and down the stairs, but tries to stay downstairs most of the time. We usually sit on the patio outside so that he can smoke. We can still do that because the winter hasn't really hit us yet. However, I suppose I'd sit out there with him even if it was freezing.

Talking to him isn't easy, as he no longer has any interests in which he can be involved. He seems to have retracted into a bit of a shell and doesn't say anything. I took a crack at talking to him about what he might want to do if his vision is not restored, but he kept shutting me down. Once he asked how he was supposed to do anything when he couldn't see. Perhaps that conversation is a bit premature, although the doctors did warn him that he might be permanently blind. He's not interested in joining a support group, but tells me he's quite happy with his own company. He doesn't seem depressed, and I hope he doesn't become that way.

One day at a time, Léonie, I say to myself, *one day at a time.* Physically, Craig is improving. His head is still a bit swollen, and he's hoping that when that subsides, his sight will improve. I hope so too.

Monday, 11 July 2011—Email

Craig is still at home, coping patiently with his impaired eyesight. He's curiously calm about it. I still visit often, but otherwise he sees hardly anyone, although he did spend this past weekend with Doug and Lindy, and I heard that Brian and Nicky visited him there. Doug and Brian doubtless find it demanding to see Craig during the week, due to the pressures of their jobs, but I know he enjoys spending the odd weekend with them. At home, Craig manages to make coffee and sandwiches, and says he's not bored, although I do wonder. At least he's not stressed, which he was when he was working; he doesn't even seem to be concerned about the shop anymore. His complacent attitude bothers me a little, but I suppose it shouldn't.

As for me, my cough has finally let up. A few weeks ago I was horribly ill with pneumonia, and my GP prescribed a strong antibiotic. I seem to be prone to picking up all sorts of bugs, but this time it was unrelenting. I finished the antibiotics, and have not coughed since. I phoned the physiotherapist to tell her I wasn't coming to see her, and I sensed the scepticism in her voice. The lung specialist probably won't buy it either, but hey, this is my body, and be it sensible or not, I've had enough of the whole medical fraternity!

Monday, 18 July 2011

Today is my mother's ninetieth birthday, and I'm pretty sure I know why Tony and I were not destined to go to Australia in July. A serious epidemic of influenza has broken out at the old age home where she stays, and no visitors are allowed onto the premises. My sister Jane says it's been very worrying for everyone. Mom was upset that no one could visit on her special birthday, but Jane managed to console her over the phone, by reminding her that we were all there in April. I was also able to speak to her on the phone. Added to that, this wouldn't have been a good time for me to go from Craig's point of view, because I feel he needs as much support as we can give him. Ian visits him as often as he can.

August 2011

The highlight of the year was a visit by Debbie and her daughters this month. They hadn't been to Africa for seven years, and although I've been to England to see them, it was wonderful to have them here, and to be able to share our lives with them for a few weeks. We had a traditional family reunion, with fun and laughter for all of us. I'm so grateful for the laughter that breaks our anxious moments. The undercurrent in this stormy sea is ever there, but the love that our family has for one another is so much stronger than any challenge that comes our way. We are very blessed.

Like most families, this one has not been without dissention over the years. With four children to my name, I suppose family disagreements are inescapable; yet I have always dreamed of an idyllic little dynasty, where everyone lives in the happy ever after, and siblings are so well matched that they're untouchable! Parents too, are beyond reproach! This, I'm afraid, is a pipe-dream, but I like to think that it just might be achievable. Perhaps my kids picked up on my delusion, for even though they've had their differences, their feuds have never been major ones, and have soon been resolved, so that now, when one of them is in big trouble, the others are rallying around him, and the whole family is united. Indeed, my pipe-dream has been realised.

With brother, Doug and sister-in-law Lindy

Craig and his sister, Debbie: July 2011

Debbie and her daughters, Kimberley and Adelaide, accompanied us to the hospital one day when Craig went for a CAT scan, making them feel a small part of what's going on in Craig's life. It was quite an experience for them, as was the chaotic traffic. I managed to break all the rules of the road that day, by doing the unthinkable, and challenging half a dozen minibus taxis, all at once! Suffice it to say that I won the contest; otherwise I would not be here to tell the tale! My grand-daughters were egging me on with, "Go for it, Gran;" my daughter was asking her brother if I always drove like a maniac; and my son was stunned to the point of rigidity, saying he was glad he couldn't see what was going down! Oh my, it was such fun! Knight Rider had nothing on me! One thing I realised that day was that this business of driving regularly in heavy traffic had turned me into a full on stunt woman!

Craig walks behind me on our visits to the hospital, giving strict instructions that I must not stop walking, because he will bump into me. I have presumed he follows my shape, but he now informs me that's not the case.

"Mother," he says, "I follow the sound of your crutch!" Oh my word! Can you imagine what that little scene must look like? The old lady hobbling along on a stick, followed by the blind man, groping his way around the corridors! What a laugh!

The Family: August 2011
Back Row: (left to right) Brian, Tony, Doug, Lindy, Craig, Ian
Centre: Léonie, Georgie
Front Row: Kimberley, Nicky, Adelaide, Debbie

I managed to get away for a week with Doug, Lindy, Debbie, Kimberley and Adelaide. We visited a game park, much to the delight of our little English family. Brian and Nicky found time to entertain them at other African venues, between quality time that Ian and I had at home with our girls. Their holiday ended all too soon, with a tearful airport departure. The most heart-wrenching thing for me was watching Debbie and Craig parting ways. They hugged as though they could not bear to let go. As their mother, I could feel their heartbeats, telling them both that this would be their last goodbye. I was watching their faces, and I perceived the deepest form of sorrow in their eyes, as though those two knew they would never see each other again on this earth. I endeavoured to define pain, and I could not.

Much later, Debbie was to write the following words as part of her tribute to her brother:

> When I see you again, Craigie, I will hug you so tightly, and thank you sincerely for being an outstanding example of humility. I have learned so much from you in the way that you lived. Your servant-hearted attitude, the way that you dealt with your "lot" has gifted us with so much food for thought: Given the same illness, the same hardship, affliction and trauma, could *we* have dealt with it so honourably? You're a hard act to follow, my boy; a leader, victorious in life, in death, and in life after death.

Debbie's holiday represented the end of a chapter in her life, and that of her younger brother. As she and her daughters passed through the gates into the departure lounge, I turned around to follow Ian and the others, with my shadow shuffling along behind me, his ears ever open to the sound of my crutch. We were back in the real world again.

Chapter 16

Saturday, 3 September 2011—extract from my journal

The scripture in my journal today says:

> The path of the just is as the shining light, that shineth more and more unto the perfect day. (Proverbs 4:18) (KJV)

I'm in my sun lounge again. The sun is bright and spring is here. The doves are sitting on branches of a tree that last month had no leaves, and now they are sprouting out, green and pretty. By next month they will have grown to full size, and the doves will be hidden from view. And so the seasons come and go. But the shining light returns daily, shining more and more unto the perfect day. For no matter what the weather, every day is a perfect reflection of God's greatness, and every season a perfect painting of His grace.

Wednesday, 14 September 2011—Email

Since the last operation, which was at the end of May this year, Craig has been very well, with no headaches, and no apparent signs of a recurrence of the tumour, although we do know that they did not remove the whole thing. Unfortunately though, his vision has not recovered. He describes it as being "blurred and as though he's in the midst of thick dust, unable to see through it." Sometimes he calls it foggy. He watches TV, and can normally get the gist of the program. He gets around the house to do odd jobs, or make himself a cup of coffee, but is uneasy in strange surroundings. It's rather difficult to figure out exactly what he can or cannot see. For instance, he's still a good back seat driver when I'm driving the car, but I have noticed that his judgement of distance isn't good. Although he can no longer work, because he can't read or use the computer, he has retained his sense of humour. I've said it before: we have to make light of many things, because if we don't, we could become miserable. Now and then I selfishly think that I am more affected by his ailment than he is. It breaks my heart to watch him shuffling along, conscious of every step he takes, and looking out for objects he might bump into. But the worst (for me) is that he must be dreadfully bored; sitting at home all day long, with only the TV and his little dog to amuse him. He shaves without cutting himself, and manages to go up and down the stairs effortlessly, although I'm told that he did fall down the stairs once. Fortunately no serious damage was done.

Today he has gone to the shop with Georgie. He's asked me to take him there on Saturday and Sunday this week, because he wants to give her a break, so I'll be driving him there and assisting for the weekend. I hope it's not a case of the blind leading the blind. When I asked him how he was coping, he said he couldn't see, but was about to find out what he could do with his impaired vision.

Next week I plan to start out on another quest with him, to make enquiries about acquiring a government disability grant. That should be almost as good fun as dealing with government hospitals. I tell myself to be positive, but I've heard a few stories about the five hour queues, and the malarkey one has to go through regarding forms, affidavits, and who knows what else. Nonetheless, we shall persevere, like the good soldiers that we are.

The next doctor's appointment at the clinic is on 7 October, when we'll get the results of an unread CAT scan and a further MRI that was done last week. Just when we were beginning to think we were familiar with all the hitches that can occur in The Hospital, we stumbled upon yet another one. Craig recently had a CAT scan, and went back a week later to see a doctor. Whilst he was in the waiting room, which *always* takes hours, I toddled off on my crutch to the X-ray department on the other side of the building, to collect the scan. By the time I returned, he'd already seen the doctor. They were busier than usual, because most of the doctors were away, and yet his wait was incredibly short. The doctor, who had never seen Craig before, decided that he was looking so well after his surgery, that he could go home, and bring the CAT scan back on his next visit, which was initially scheduled for the end of November. I was fed up that I hadn't made it back to the consulting room in time. I felt that the doctor should have told Craig to re-join the queue, and wait until he got the CAT scan, then bring it for him to look at. By the time a doctor gets to see that scan, it will be out of date. No one can say I don't know what frustration is! Before the last op, we had made a booking for an MRI in August, but unscheduled surgery was subsequently performed in May. We didn't cancel the MRI appointment, because we've learned to be smart in that place. If you have an appointment, you keep it, because you may never get another chance to get into that overly popular MRI machine. So last week I took Craig for the MRI, and now he will have two scans to show the doctor next month. CAT scans and MRI's cannot be compared with one another, as they show completely different aspects of the body part in question, but at least there will be two views, albeit the tumour could change before Craig sees a doctor. The latest scan is not yet in our hands, and we sincerely hope that it won't be amongst the many items that do the disappearing trick in The Hospital. By a miracle, I managed to bring the November appointment at the clinic forward to 7 October. I think the gentleman at the appointments desk knows my face, and it wouldn't surprise me if he tells his co-worker that they'd better not mess with that Mama! That would be a joke—that fellow doesn't take any flak from anyone. I marched up to 456, the neuro ward, and managed to reclaim all Craig's previous scans, which they'd refused to let us have when he was discharged after his surgery. We were told they were government property. Since the government has an alarming habit of losing things, there was a chance we'd never see them again, but lo and behold, Mother Hen got her hands on them. Since this ordeal began, I've learned how to win friends and influence people, and I've never read the book.

In the past three years, Craig has had three major brain operations and seven weeks of daily radiation, all of which have involved me running around the countryside habitually. During that time I've had a hip replacement and a lung biopsy, and am now due for another hip replacement, so it's been a trying time, but I have every confidence that we will come through it unscathed. The mind-boggling fact is that Craig and I have both had major surgery a number of times and never once have our operations clashed with one another. God has looked after us both, and has enabled us to look after each other. Craig will be forty next month and we didn't know if he would reach thirty-seven.

Tuesday, 27 September 2011

Today involved hours of waiting in queues, applying for the disability grant, which turned out to be slightly less complicated than expected, although rather frustrating, like all government departments. We hung about for over two hours just to get a form to fill out. I had checked the Health Department's website, but the forms are not available on-line—one has to physically go and fetch them. Then one has to go back to hand them in with the rest of the requirements. It's a bit like living in the Stone Age!

After filling in the initial form, we went to the police station to get it certified, and then to the bank, for statements. They also need documentation from the neurosurgeons, so we'll get that next month.

My weekend with Craig in the shop went well, and he's been there with Georgie for the last week or so, attempting to help. Poor fellow can barely see what he's doing, but he battles on. I think he's finding being in the shop stressful, but I can't get involved in that; he has to do what he has to do.

I've been to see the orthopaedic surgeon and a physician, so am set for hip surgery on 8 November. I'm not looking forward to it, but at least I know what to expect, having had this done twice before. I pray that Craig stays well, because I won't be of much help for the rest of this year.

Friday, 7 October 2011

This was another exasperating day. The consulting surgeon at The Hospital was unknown to both Craig and me, and completely unacquainted with Craig's history. The so-called records files never tell anyone anything, and although Craig tried to fill the doctor in as to what's been happening to him over the past three years, he didn't seem particularly interested. He signed the form for the disability grant, and sent Craig home with another appointment for March next year. He wouldn't issue a referral for an MRI prior to the March appointment, which effectively means that Craig will have to see a surgeon in March, without any evidence of the state of the tumour. At that point, they will probably send him to book an MRI. The machine will either be booked for weeks, or broken, so another wait will ensue; but with loads of luck, Craig's scan will be done by the middle of the year, and only then will he be able to make a booking to see another surgeon. As the notorious Beatles used to sing, "Here we come again, yeah, yeah!" I was not impressed with that surgeon. I detected that his view was "Let's see if this man makes it to March next year." I cannot abide by characters like that.

Friday, 2nd November 2011—Email

This will be my last update before my surgery next week. Once again I'll be out of commission for a couple of months—on two crutches for at least six weeks, and then back to one; the good news being that I will be able to throw away these crutches once and for all early next year. I've been walking with one crutch for the past seven months, so this will be like Heaven! With all that has transpired in my middle son's life, I haven't had time to attend to myself, but am now in a pretty bad way, and this surgery can't wait any longer.

As for Craig, he's well, although his poor vision is unchanging. He can't drive, read, or use the computer, which can be rather frustrating, but he remains uncomplaining. I think he has learned to appreciate the value of life, and he copes well. He's still working in the shop and although he can't do everything he used to do, he's adjusted well. We keep going back and forth to the hospital for various reasons, the latest of which has been to get his eyes tested. He has worn glasses since he was a teenager, but hasn't had an eye test for a long time. When the brain tumour appeared and damaged his optic nerves, he didn't think of getting his eyes tested again, but recently started wondering if stronger spectacles might help improve his vision. The eye clinic was a new venture for us, and like most of the other departments, the waiting was exactly the same. The second crocheted blanket is coming along nicely! We collected his new long distance glasses today. There doesn't seem to be any noticeable difference in his vision, which confirms that a lot of harm has been done to the optic nerves. Next week he'll be getting reading glasses, and is hoping that these will enable him to use the computer and read again.

Craig celebrated his fortieth birthday on 30 October. I opted not to share his birthday this year, because I wanted it to be his day alone. We had a quiet evening braai (barbecue) at Doug and Lindy's, marred only by the ever present cognizance that it could be his last birthday. We almost lost him before his thirty seventh birthday and every birthday since then has been a bonus.

We were at the hospital today, and I couldn't help noticing the magnificent jacaranda trees all around. The complex is on a hill, overlooking a portion of the city. The first time I went there, I remember gazing out of the window of the ward, and looking down on a resplendent mass of purple jacarandas. They're blooming again. Craig's first surgery took place at 11:00 a.m. on the eleventh day of the eleventh month of that year and here we are, three years later, at the same time of year in two thousand and eleven. I'm not superstitious, but there does seem to be something strange about these elevens.

Monday, 7 November 2011

Having spent two more days with Craig in a crowded waiting room at the Pensions Office, he was eventually awarded his disability grant, which although meagre, will provide him with enough cash for his personal requirements. I'm pleased to have that sorted out before I go into hospital.

I hear that Craig's been spending a couple of weekends a month with Doug and Lindy, which is wonderful for him. I think Brian and Nicky sometimes visit as well. It's encouraging to know that my boys are together, but I suppose I will never stop worrying about what Craig is getting up to. He shouldn't be drinking, but I know he does. Nicky celebrated her thirtieth birthday on Saturday, and Craig definitely drank too much, which didn't go down well with Ian and me, but we remained silent. We started filling his glass with coke, and he didn't even notice the difference. He can't afford to drink at home, so I'm consoled by that fact.

Chapter 17

On 30 November 2011, Craig came to live with Ian and me. We'd been telling him for months that he would be welcome to come home if the need arose, but it must have been a very difficult move for him to make. Georgie could no longer maintain the shop in Alberton, so at the end of October, with the help of Doug and Brian, she moved the business to Benoni. Each day she'd go out marketing, while Craig stayed in the shop, waiting for customers who never came. I couldn't help because I was house-bound, due to my recent surgery. Once again Nurse Ian had taken two weeks' leave to look after me, so each day he would go down to the new shop to take lunch for Craig, who insisted he didn't need any, but he ate it anyway! He would sit there all day with one of their dogs. He struggled on in the shop until the end of November, but it was obvious that he could no longer work, nor stay at home alone. He was very concerned about his little dog, Bam, but it was unfeasible for Ian and me to take him, due to his intense dislike of other dogs, including ours; so regrettably Craig had to part with him. There was so much sadness in his life, and although my heart kept on breaking, I knew that Ian and I would have to pull together to take care of our son. We had no idea what the future held, but we did know that we'd been tasked with a heavy burden. In retrospect, we cared for Craig with love, and wholly by the grace of God. Not knowing the future is a blessing, because that knowledge could either cripple us, or make us complacent. Already, as human beings, we take so much for granted, and I think that's a very dangerous thing to do. What we have can be taken away in an instant. When our boy came to stay with us, there was still hope in my heart that he would survive this horrible disease. I was probably alone in my reasoning, but I needed to hold on to something. Later on I would be led graciously into a place of acceptance.

As I hobbled around on crutches, minor frustrations became the order of the day. Craig groped his way around the house, unable to do anything constructive. The blindness, however, was not his biggest drawback. Under constant threat of the monster in his head, he was ever aware of its implications. The pressure on his brain made him feel ill, and he said his whole body ached. The permanent dull headache often escalated to severe pain, and he had no energy at all. He would try to be cheerful, but this was becoming increasingly difficult, and I kept trying to convince myself that things would get better. One day I was praying about it and I asked God to help us to live the moment, because we didn't know how many more moments we'd have. That was the day I knew that I would call this book "Living the Moment." Craig was living the moment. I think he'd been doing that ever since he was diagnosed. I'd be forever grateful for the time we'd been afforded to spend with our son, and for whatever time was still ahead of us. Life is unpredictable, but looking out for rainbows seemed like a good idea. There's an old song which goes, "Look for the silver lining, whene'r a cloud appears in the sky; remember somewhere the sun is shining . . ." I honestly believe if we do that when we're in big trouble, things will become a little easier to handle. Laughter is good for the soul too. We need to do more of that.

Ian went back to work at the beginning of December, by which time Craig and I managed to help each other cope with our respective disabilities. The blind leading the crippled scenario worked quite well. We began to joke about one another, and the moments started lightening up a bit; in fact, it must have been amusing to watch the two of us, an odd couple indeed. One day I asked him to plug the computer into the wall, because I couldn't bend down to reach the socket. He couldn't see what he was doing, so it was me giving useless instructions, and him fumbling around in the dark! What a performance!

I'm saying, "A bit to the left; no that's too much; no higher; okay, now shove!"

And he's saying, "There's no need to shout—I'm blind, not deaf!" What a movie that would make!

Because I was on crutches, I couldn't carry anything, so I would cruise into the kitchen in the mornings and switch on the kettle, which Ian had thoughtfully filled before leaving for work. I would rest one crutch on the table and make the tea. Craig would have to find the milk and sugar. Once the tea was made, I would pick up the second crutch and totter through the main lounge into the sun lounge, where I would ease my way into a chair. Craig would pick up both cups of tea, and follow the sound of my rather loud steps. I would worry that he might trip, but he never did. He would bring me my cup of tea, and then shuffle around to his own chair. All this took quite a while, but after all was said and done, we did have all day! Then we'd chat about anything that did not involve our incapacities. If the phone rang in the adjacent room, that was another story! When Ian came home from work, he would do all the things we hadn't managed to do between us, including making dinner.

Monday, 5 December 2011—Email

Craig's headaches seem to be getting worse. I'm almost trying to put myself into denial, for fear of cracking up. To add to our woes, our eleven year old Beagle dog is nearing the end of her days. She lost a huge amount of weight in a week. A few thousand rand of vet bills later, we were told she has liver and kidney failure, and has now lost almost half her body weight in about five weeks. She's not in pain, but she won't eat, and has suddenly gone from a lively, happy dog, to a listless little creature. It's awful, but Ian can't let go and is now feeding her Pro Nutro porridge with a syringe. He knows we will soon have to have her put down, but she's his baby, and he's battling with it. The big picture is that she's only a dog, but watching her and Craig all day long takes its toll on me. What a blessing that I'm recovering well from my surgery, because I don't have the stamina to worry about my health as well.

Tuesday, 6 December 2011—Email

Watching our son deteriorating this way is torture. He has slept most of the day today. He's never hungry, but he does eat at least one good meal a day. I feel utterly helpless. I don't know what to think or feel anymore. This is so different to anything else we've been through. He's getting very forgetful and keeps repeating himself. He feels his way around the house in constant discomfort and pain. He says he's not stressed, but I think he must be. His whole body aches continually; he says it feels like it's in his bones and his muscles. Even his toes hurt. He has talked about dying, and he sometimes gives the impression that he wishes he could hasten that.

My quilting class ladies are having a little Christmas brunch tomorrow morning, and one of the ladies is picking me up. This is the first time I've been out since the op, and I could do with the break. It means I have to leave Craig on his own, which he keeps assuring me is fine. He does manage, but I'm not feeling too good about it. However, I know that I'll have to go back to work in the new year, and there will be two days a week that he's alone, so I'm going to have to get used to it.

Friday, 9 December 2011

We had a bad night with Craig last night. He was calling out, and Ian found him wandering around the house looking for the toilet at 2:00 a.m. The previous night he'd turned the wrong way, and set off the house alarm. Last night Ian led him to the bathroom, but he was disorientated and wanted to go outside for a cigarette. He swears that smoking eases his headaches. Ian waited up till he'd had his cigarette and got him back to bed. An hour later, the same thing happened, and once more he had to go out for a smoke. As non-smokers, this is uncomfortable for Ian and me, but we know how badly he needs his cigarettes, and we no longer try to stop him. However, I think we'll have to put a stop to these midnight stints. It's interesting to note that Craig once wrote on Facebook that smoking is probably what caused his tumour, though he tells us it's too late to stop now. One Internet website says that no links have been found between glioblastoma and smoking, so the question remains unanswered.

After the midnight smoking escapade, neither Ian nor I could get back to sleep. Ian gets up at 4:30 a.m. every day to go to work, and went off looking like a zombie this morning. At 7:00 a.m. I was still lying in bed, when I heard Craig calling. Off I went on my crutches, to find him sitting on the kitchen floor, battling to get up. He said his head was hurting and he was dizzy. I talked him through it and he managed to get up. We had a cup of tea and he seemed okay, but I was pretty shaken and looking for sympathy, so I phoned Doug to tell him what was going on. At 9:00 a.m. Doug and Lindy arrived. Lindy, being an ex-nursing sister, had a few theories, and it was ultimately established that Craig had taken some strong pain pills, which we supposed had caused the crisis. I have now confiscated his medication, and told him I will give it to him on request. The concern is that he may not remember he has taken it, and subsequently take too much. He is aware that he suffers from short term memory loss, and he's quite happy for me to control his dosage. It's sad that in some respects we have to treat him like a child, but he does acknowledge the problem.

Monday, 12 December 2011

Today Ian went flying and Doug came over to fetch his brother and me to for Sunday lunch at their house. I haven't been to church since my hip surgery because I can't drive, so it was nice to get out. Craig is more receptive when he's with other people, so it was good for him too. I often get frustrated with him because I feel he plays on my emotions. I hate to say this, but he will hang his head down and say he's feeling sick, but if somebody arrives here, he's suddenly not so sick after all. I don't know if he's seeking my sympathy, or if he's putting on a show for other people, but whatever it is, it's getting me down, and there are times when I want to throw something at him. I have to remind myself of how ill he is. If he is overplaying it, I have to forgive him, and ask myself what I would do in his situation. Because I'm the one who's with him the most, I guess he can be himself with me, but I'm afraid he irritates me at times. Perhaps this is only a phase; I don't know, but I'm finding it hard to deal with. I don't think he would ever deliberately upset me, but he certainly uses me to offload his frustrations. There is no doubt that he is ill. I'm forced to learn tolerance of a rather complex nature. Trying to identify with what he's going through is complicated in itself, but empathising with him is the test. Here is a man who for almost forty years led a normal life. He is now largely confined to his parents' home, with little or nothing to occupy himself on a daily basis, save watching a bit of TV, which he can barely see, listening to the radio, eating, which rarely appeals to him, and sleeping, probably to pass the time away. He enjoys spending the odd weekend with his brothers, but friends and family aren't able to entertain him continually. Georgie's been to our home for dinner once or twice, but other than that, we've seen little of her. She's told us she'll be spending Christmas with her daughters.

Tuesday, 27 December 2011

Christmas Day was quiet, but lovely to share lunch with our two younger boys. Doug and Lindy were away. Last year we had about sixteen friends and family for lunch, with fun and laughter, so this was different; but we brought out the family silver and ate a traditional meal. Craig refused a glass of wine—he hasn't touched a drop of alcohol since he's been with us. He says it makes him sick. He went to lie down after lunch, and when Brian left, Ian and I did the same. The last couple of days have been quiet, a visitor popping in now and again, but not much else. Craig had a strange turn the day after Christmas, shaking and perspiring. I don't know if it was some sort of mild seizure, but it didn't last long and he's been fine since then. Recently, he's been back on his prescribed medication, which he hadn't taken for months. It's basically a seizure preventative, which he said he didn't need, but because he's not well, and we don't know what's going on inside his head, we felt it would be best for him to take the medication. His next neurosurgeon's appointment is almost three months away, so we feel he should take the necessary precautions against a would-be attack. Nothing is guaranteed; we can only hope it's the right thing to do.

Thursday, 29 December 2011

Our dear little Beagle dog, Baguette, died today. She was best friend to our Siberian Husky, Ice. My philosophy of seeking a positive in every negative situation has surely been put to the test.

Saturday, 31 December 2011

People can be so inspiring in times such as these. It amazes me that folk I've never met have been sending me emails of encouragement and hope. One friend will pass my emails on to friends of hers, and I get messages from people who never heard of the Edwards family until Craig became ill. Such a person is a man called Ken in Australia. Not only has he sent emails, but he also sent a book called "How to Outsmart your Cancer," which he was hopeful might be of benefit to Craig. He has phoned me and we are now friends who will probably never meet, yet friends who have a common interest, a family member with this dreaded disease called cancer. Craig was overwhelmed that anyone would do such a kind thing. In his desperation for a cure, he keeps asking me if I've read the book yet. It's a thick book and I'm labouring to read it, because with all that's taking place, settling down to read is tricky. I'm trying;

I'm really trying. I don't know if it will help our son, but I'm sure it will help someone. I believe there's a reason it came into my hands, and I'm very grateful to Ken. What a compassionate man! There are many others like him; they don't all send books, but they pray and encourage us. I can feel the anguish in their hearts when they can find no words to express their sadness on reading about Craig's misfortune.

Even though he can still hold a normal conversation, make a joke, and engage in an argument, his body movements are slow. He shuffles around, mostly looking at the ground, and I don't think it's because of his eyesight. When walking, he has a tendency to cup his hands for no apparent reason, and when I asked him about it, he replied that it's the way he is now and he can't help it. His bladder seems to be weakening. With his slow movement, he's had one or two minor accidents, and my heart cries for him when he has to come and tell me, because he can't see to wipe up the mess, and he can't wash his own clothes. There's no such thing as "hurry up and get ready". If he's going anywhere, I have to start nagging him to get dressed two hours beforehand. He'll say it's too early to get ready. There's no urgency in anything. He will consistently be late, and then he'll joke and say it's my fault. He listens to his radio and tries to send messages from his cell phone in response to radio competitions, but he can't see the buttons on the cell phone, so he calls me to do it for him. I get frustrated with this, but I can't say no. He's so determined to win a fortune from one of these calls, and since he has nothing else with which to occupy himself, I can't refuse. He keeps asking us to buy him lotto tickets, and when I asked him what he would do with the winnings, he replied that he would find the best neurosurgeon in the world. I wished I hadn't asked. He sleeps a lot, although I don't know if he's actually sleeping or passing the time away. If friends visit me, he usually comes and sits with us. He enjoys company other than mine. It must be uninspiring for a man his age to have no company, other than that of his mother on a daily basis. He looks forward to seeing his brothers, but they are restricted to weekend visiting, due to their job commitments.

When he was managing his shop, he saw many people each day, so this has been a drastic change for him in all respects.

I don't know what to pray for anymore. My son has no quality of life, and yet he's not moaning about it. I want so much for him to be healed. I want him to be like he used to be. I want to turn back the clock and halt time. But I can't. Why is it that I feel an urgency to finish the crocheted blanket?

Chapter 18

2012 was ushered in with force for the Edwards family. Ian turned seventy on 12 January. Twelve of us went out for dinner, and a good time was had by all. When Ian took Georgie home afterwards, she mentioned that she was looking for a job.

On the Friday after that, our grandson, David, came to spend the weekend with us. David is the son of Brian's first wife. He was brought into our family as a baby, and immediately bonded with Ian and me. He is now sixteen years old and I'm very happy to say that he visits us as regularly as possible. I love it when he comes. He indulges this granny like no other teenage boy I know. On Friday night he and I played cards. That little bit of light-hearted entertainment did me the world of good. I made a point of cheating, purely for the delight in watching his face whenever I did so.

"Gra a n!" he would exclaim and I would go, "What?"

"You cheated!"

"I did not!"

"Yes, you did, Gran."

I would grin and say, "No, David, that's not cheating. You're allowed to do that when you get older!"

He would look at me and shake his head, then we would both burst out laughing. Did we start again? Not a chance! He would typically win anyway, so I had to have my moment. Would it not be wonderful if all our moments were like that?

The plan was that we would take David home on Sunday afternoon, but on Saturday Craig took a turn for the worse, and poor David was subjected to some rather disturbing occurrences. Ian and I were up half the night attending to our son and we made the decision to take him to Casualty at The Hospital on Sunday morning. We arranged to take David home first, and having dropped him off, we spent the whole day in Casualty. Over the next few months, David and his mother visited Craig at our home a couple of times.

At the hospital, we managed to secure a wheelchair, and a very obliging porter wheeled Craig to see a nurse, whose job it was to do a screening process, to asses who was eligible to see a doctor in that hospital. Some patients are referred to smaller clinics. Craig already has his "admission ticket", the priceless Blue Book, but he still had to go through the formalities relating to seeing any type of doctor in a state hospital. The nurse took his blood pressure and did a sugar test. Everything was normal. The only part of his body that's not normal is his brain—how sad that is, considering that the brain dictates what the whole body does. Having to go to Casualty is a pain in the neck, but it's the only way to get in if you don't have "an appointment".

We could tell by the crowd in the waiting room that we'd be there for hours. Ian wheeled Craig down to the smoking area a few times, while I kept his place in the queue. Casualty must be the furthest department from the smoking area, so Ian did some walking that day. Craig would never have been able to walk around that place. His co-ordination was in confusion, so he couldn't even feel his way around, but the wheelchair worked well. At about 3:00 p.m., our turn came and we saw a very young GP, who hadn't a clue about Craig's condition. She promptly gave him a referral to see a neurosurgeon the next day. When I explained to her that they don't consult on Mondays, she looked at me patronizingly.

"They are here every day," she asserted.

"Doctor," I said, amiably, but with conviction, "We've been coming here regularly for three years. The neurosurgeons only consult on Fridays."

"You'll find them in the clinic," she said.

"I know that," I continued calmly, "but that particular clinic is only open on Fridays."

She opened her mouth, but I carried on talking, as I do. Both father and son were scrutinising the floor.

"Doctor, this man can't wait till Friday. He's seriously ill. With respect, I think I'm more familiar with this tumour than you are. He could have a seizure at any minute. Last time that happened, he nearly died."

Ian sat there with his mouth half open, but he knew I was a past master at sweet-talking the medical fraternity in that hospital.

"So what do you want me to do?" she asked.

"Don't refer him to the clinic," I requested, "Please give him a letter of access to ward 456. The surgeons do their rounds from 8.30 a.m. each day. Once we get in there, we'll wait for one of them to complete his morning visits to patients."

"And you think he'll simply stop and see your son after that?" she asked in disbelief.

"Yes, Doctor," I replied, "I do."

Craig didn't intervene, but I could see he was starting to get embarrassed. However, he was desperate to see a surgeon and appreciated my persuasive manner. I was amused by the referral the doctor gave us. It was addressed to a "whom it may concern" neurosurgeon and effectively asked him to see Mr Edwards on Monday, in "'either the clinic or the ward," whichever suited best. Clearly, she did not believe me. One thing I'd picked up very quickly in that place was that both medical practitioners and staff were assigned to their departments, and their departments only, having little or no knowledge of what went on outside their areas. This was not the first, nor the last time this happened. I was convinced that I was more familiar with the general run of the place than most of them were.

It was a long way from Casualty back to the car park. En route we came upon ward 456, where Craig had spent so many days and weeks in the course of the past three years. On approaching that familiar dented door frame, I suddenly felt the urge to make a turn. I looked at my watch—4:00 p.m. We'd been there almost the whole day. Visiting hours were from 3:00 p.m. to 5:00 p.m., so there wouldn't be any objection to our walking in.

"Make a left!" I said to Ian.

"What's happening?" a bewildered Craig inquired.

"We're going to visit your ward," I grinned.

"What for?" my equally bewildered husband added, "This is stupid. I want to go home."

I carried on grinning. "I'm going to look for a proper doctor, guys."

"Mom," Craig said, "The doctors *never* go into the wards at visiting hours. They're scared stiff of people like you!"

"He's right," Ian said, "The last thing they want is to be bombarded with patients' relatives.

"Please Ian," I said, "Just make a left."

I'm not a nagging wife, just very persuasive! Ian obeyed. We were immediately confronted by half a dozen nursing staff.

"Mr Craig! Mr Craig! What are you doing in a wheelchair? Oh, Mr Craig!"

My heart had so many cracks in it by then that I thought it would surely split in half that day. One nurse came up to us and gave me a hug.

"Is Gentleman Craig sick?" she enquired, "Are you admitting him?"

"No," I replied, "But he does need to see a doctor."

Craig chipped in, "I've told her that's impossible."

The familiar face of the senior nurse appeared. "No, it's not," she smiled, "There's a crisis in ICU and one of the neurosurgeons is in there. She'll be out shortly."

"God's favour again," I whispered.

We found a couple of seats in the nurses' station, from where I could see into the intensive care unit. Relatives were gathered around a bed. They were obviously crying. *Oh dear God!* I thought. Someone was either dead or dying! A nurse drew the curtain around them, and the young lady doctor emerged from the room. I didn't tell Craig what I'd witnessed. I knew this could be us one day. It was horrible. The doctor walked into the nurses' station, removing her gloves, and wiping her brow. She sat down behind the counter, talking softly to the senior nursing sister. She obviously hadn't seen us. Someone gave her a glass of water. This didn't seem to be a good time, I thought; her patient was probably dead. This wasn't a good time. Then she rose, picking up a file, and turned to leave. The sister looked over at us and nodded. As the young lady doctor walked around to the other side of the counter, she momentarily glanced our way.

"Doctor," I called softly, "Craig's here."

She stopped in her tracks. "Craig? A wheelchair?" She walked over to him, extending her hand to shake his, but he couldn't see it.

"He's pretty much blind," I said.

Her face was sad, but Craig beamed.

"You sound like the one who did my last op. Thanks, you did a good job."

She put out her hand to hold mine. Once again, yes, once again, I was reading a neurosurgeon's eyes. She had a chat with Craig, then told Ian and me that he would have to come for an assessment at the clinic on Friday. Of course, he didn't have an appointment, but she took his Blue Book and made one for him. That was a first. I'd never seen a doctor do that before. I was under the impression that only the officious fellow at the clinic reception could do that. In the meantime the doctor told us to make sure Craig ate three meals a day for the next few days, which was a bit of a joke, because that hadn't happened for weeks. She changed the medication dosage slightly, and said he could have as many painkillers as he needed. We never saw her again, but I expect she's somewhere there, furthering the cause of saving lives. What a lovely lady.

Tuesday, 17 January 2012

Craig's having a better day today. Whilst he's lucid most of the time, he tends to see things that aren't there and what is there, he sees in the wrong place, which is problematical, because he wants to put items on tables that are a foot away, and he bumps into things because he thinks they are further away than they actually are. We have to hold his hand much of the time, or otherwise prompt him on where to go. He's ever so slow, so it's quite a laborious process. He keeps wanting to go outside to smoke which is such a mission that we let him smoke in the sun lounge with the door and windows open. He certainly has not forgotten how to smoke. However, he often cannot light his cigarette, which is so sad. He puts it in his mouth, flicks the lighter and then holds it inches away from the cigarette. It's hopeless. I never thought I'd see Ian lighting a cigarette for him—he's so anti-smoking—but we can learn from this. The strange thing is that since his sudden degeneration a couple of days ago, his headaches seem to be better. It's as if the tumour has shifted away from the place which causes pain, to other places which cause different malfunctions. We don't know what to expect next, but we were told some time ago that things like this could happen. Craig has been having hallucinations lately, insisting that there are trees growing in the lounge, and plants all over the place. In the underground parking lot, he was convinced we were parked in the mountains and the next day, on the way to Georgie's house, where I left him for the morning because I had to go to work, he swore there was water everywhere on the road. I told him it must have been raining and he was satisfied with that. He periodically says he can see people who aren't there and although he's not alarmed by them, he says they are very irritating. Today, however, he hasn't seen anything strange. He usually eats well at night, but has little during the day. However, he is now doing what the doctor ordered and having his three meals daily, so perhaps that's why he's a bit better today. Yesterday I left him sitting in the sun lounge while I was on the phone in the bedroom. Martha, our part-time house-keeper, came through and told me he'd gone outside and was calling me. He was way down the garden, and said he was trying to find his way back to the house. I asked why he had gone outside, and he replied that he had wanted to go to his bedroom, but stepped out of the front door by mistake and couldn't find his way back into the house. I obviously can't leave him by an open door. He short term memory loss is worsening and he asks the same questions over and over—like, "what time are we going out?" and "where did you say we were going?" Through all this, he will sit in the lounge and conduct an intelligent conversation, even making jokes. We watch quiz programmes on TV and he answers many of the questions. Because of his blindness and poor co-ordination, I've resorted to giving him a spoon with which to eat his dinner. Quite often he tries to lift food off the table because he sees the plate in the wrong place. Periodically, when he picks up the food, his hand wanders to the side of his face, inches away from his mouth, but his mouth is open, waiting to eat the food. I tend to push the food onto the spoon without him realising it, purely to hurry him up a bit. He tries so hard to do it himself.

At night I'm the hardened nurse, dishing out medication, making him clean his teeth without spitting out on the floor, and instructing him on his new toilet procedure. It breaks my heart, but to date he is retaining his dignity. We practically have to tuck him into bed, and as long as he has his Christmas present, a little Walka TV, which he is well capable of switching off and on and changing channels, he's quite happy. He lies in bed with his glasses on, and yet I have never found them still on when he wakes up, so I guess that part of his brain is still fine. Had he been like he is today, we wouldn't have gone to Casualty, but we couldn't risk another bad night like the one we had, or at worst, a seizure. This tumour is not is easy to understand. Ian is taking a day's leave on Friday, so we can go to the hospital together, because I can't do the wheelchair thing; so it's a whole new ball game now.

Tuesday, 24 January 2012—Email

I'm doing well after my hip replacement, and am now walking without crutches. I feel like a "Look, Ma, no hands" kid, having used one or two crutches since March last year. My surgeon was pleased with my progress and I feel like a new person.

The visit to the clinic on Friday was disconcerting. We saw our friend the Indian surgeon, whom I am always delighted to see, but the news is not good. After a brief consultation with Craig, the surgeon asked to speak to Ian and me alone. Craig later told me that he was upset about that, even though he agreed to it. He felt that it was his body and his fate we were discussing, and he is not a child. I agreed with him, but emphasised that the doctor felt that it would be better for us to explain the prognosis to him, rather than him hearing it from a doctor. Be that as it may, I promised Craig that on his next visit in February, he could speak to the surgeon personally. This was tricky, because Craig is an adult, but his mind is definitely deteriorating, and the Indian surgeon felt that we were better acquainted with our son's mental state than he was, and were therefore better equipped to relay the bad news to him. What he told us was that he was amazed that Craig has lived for so long with this type of tumour. However, because of his rapid decline in recent weeks, he felt certain he was nearing the end of his life. Further surgery would make him much worse, and he should go home and spend the time that he has with his family who love him. We did relay this to Craig when we got home, but he was still adamant that the doctor should have told him himself. Perhaps so, I'm not sure. Craig asked the surgeon if he could have another MRI and the surgeon agreed, although we felt that this was merely to give Craig confirmation of the prognosis. What an unpleasant day that turned out to be.

I'm almost coming to a place of acceptance. What a strange feeling. Nursing has become second nature to me now, and we can no longer leave Craig alone. The only time I manage to get out is to go to work twice a week, when we find someone to care for him. Friends pop in to see me and they don't know what to say. I see Edith frequently and the look in her eyes says it all. My friend who lost her daughter knows all about it, but she too has no words to say to me.

Added to all this tension, a week ago Ian's car was stolen from our yard at two o'clock in the morning. The thieves broke the gate lock, and wheeled the car out, even though it had a good gear lock, immobilizer and alarm system. Ian and I had swopped cars, so this was the same car that a fellow bashed into last year. It was an old car, but was in excellent shape. What the insurers will pay out is by no means sufficient to buy another vehicle, so that will have to be put on hold for the time being. As if this wasn't enough, on Sunday I discovered that someone has fraudulently withdrawn money from my bank account. The bank official explained to me how this is done, and I can only say that nothing is safe these days. I will get the money back from the bank, but the inconvenience is very annoying. It has all been a bit much; Ian and I are both taking strain. However, we gotta keep our chins up, because there ain't much else we can do! It will come right; it always does, even though it's not an easy road. Count your blessings, Léonie; like how good it is to have Craig at home, where we can keep an eye on him, and not have to keep our ears half open at night, anticipating a phone call with not so good news. It's good to laugh at his silly sense of humour, even though his jokes are generally about himself and his debilitating ailment. Because he can't see, I hold both his hands and walk backwards, leading him along. That's right, no sooner had I discarded the crutches, than I began walking backwards! As Craig is pulled along by his mother, he starts singing that ridiculous song he's heard on the radio—"Every day I'm shuffling . . ." He jokes with Martha, asking her where he can buy dagga to smoke because he's heard it has medicinal content and is particularly good for headaches. Dagga (cannabis) is an illegal drug, but then indubitably, so is heroine and there's an abundance of that in Craig's painkillers, so he wants to know why he can't have dagga as well! I'm not sure if we should be laughing at that, but we do.

Sunday, 5 February 2012

I made notes in my diary today. Writing doesn't appear to be what I really feel inclined to do right now. I'm leaving the notes as they are because they depict my inner feelings. I'm falling apart, and I don't see how a person can write a book when she's falling apart.

- For the time being, I'm doing my office work at home because there's no one to look after Craig.
- I need to find a new church. Maybe that will lift my spirits. I feel badly let down by the other church. No point in elaborating.
- Chronic headaches today. Co-ordination, balance bad. Says his neck aches and he feels as though the tumour is pushing his eyes out—they appear to be bulging, he says. His feet hurt, everything hurts.
- Short term memory is getting bad. Keeps asking the same questions, over and over again. "What day are we going for the MRI?" "Tuesday."
- "When do I see the doctor?" "Friday." Twenty times a day.
- "I need to ask the doctor something. I'm telling you this now, because I know I'll forget." "What do you want to ask?" "Oh, I've forgotten already." "Is it about the pills?" "I don't know, but I want to ask about the pills too. How many can I take?" "It's okay, I have a list of questions to ask the doctor. That's on the list." "When do I see the doctor?" "Friday."

Chapter 19

It was during January that I put the finishing touches to the crocheted blanket. One ordinarily feels a sense of gratification on completion of such a project, but tears came to my eyes when I held it up to show my husband. He always compliments me profusely on my handiwork, but this time I felt only a hollow throb in my soul.

"He'll never even see it," I said.

"But he can feel it," Ian reassured me, "And he'll appreciate that you made it for him, which is more to the point."

"But it's summer, and by the time the winter comes . . ." I couldn't complete the sentence, because I was crying. No, I couldn't complete the sentence because I couldn't face hearing myself say that Craig may not be here for the winter. I couldn't face the fact that he may never use the blanket. Of course, it wasn't about the blanket at all. It was the concept of the blanket that brought the reality home to me. My Craigie was dying. My baby boy's life was nearly over.

"Give him the blanket," Ian said.

I took it to him. "Remember the blanket I was knitting for you Craig?"

"Crocheting," he corrected.

How many times had I corrected him on that subject? And now, in his critical moments, he remembered. I smiled as I gave him the blanket, and I felt the love in his heart as he took it from me; but I knew that by the next day he would have forgotten all about it. The weather was too warm to use it, so I put it away in his cupboard and attempted to forget about it. If anything was a labour of love, that blanket was, but after all was said and done, it was only a blanket.

In early February Ian and I took Craig back to the hospital for his final MRI. Previously, he'd gone through that procedure easily, but this time it was a terrible ordeal for him and we knew we could never again subject him to that. He had to wait over half an hour after having the contrast medium injected into his body and he sat there shivering, from cold, or nerves, or both. They had taken his glasses away, so he couldn't see at all, but they did allow Ian and me to sit with him while he was waiting outside that freezing room where they kept the scanner. By the time he came out of it, he looked dreadful. He admitted, for the first time, that he'd battled to get through the process, showing us once again how very ill he was. I couldn't help thinking about his first MRI, when he was joking about his magnetic personality and repeating the story about the wheelchair that had been forcefully drawn to the magnetic scanner. We'd all been laughing that day, never dreaming for one minute that a little over three years down the line the state of affairs would be so different.

A few days later, we took him for his final visit to the neuro clinic. We saw the disabled surgeon again. He did no more than glance at the MRI scan. I had read the report while we were sitting in the waiting room. The tumour now measured 7 cm x 8.1 cm, which was almost as big as it was three years ago, before the first operation. And it was still growing. The surgeon sat with the three of us and told Craig they had done whatever they could for him, and that his life was now completely in God's hands. He had the most wonderfully gentle manner, and after we assured him that we knew that God was in control, he spoke to us about spiritual matters, making it so much easier for Craig to accept that the end was near. We've encountered numerous administrational issues in that hospital, but I am indebted to those doctors for the good work they are doing and the care they gave our son. The surgeon issued a prescription for five monthly repeats of his medication, but yet again I read his eyes, which told me he was not expecting Craig to live anywhere near that length of time. Someone asked me why Craig was taking medication. I explained that all he has is something to stop seizures, steroids to take the swelling off the brain, thus easing the pressure, and painkillers. There's nothing to get rid of the tumour, nothing to prolong his life. The medication is purely to make him a little more comfortable. The surgeon gave me his mobile phone number, saying we were welcome to ring him if we needed any further assistance. One day I will ring him. I think he deserves to know the final outcome.

One evening Ian had to go to a meeting and I was alone with Craig. I took him outside for a cigarette, leaving him standing on the concrete slab by the back door. Then I went inside to get something, and on hearing a loud thud, I charged back to investigate. I found him lying on the concrete, unable to get up. That would be the last time I was to take him outside. I struggled to help him up by getting him to hold on to the security gate at the back of the door. His hand was bleeding profusely and he was badly shaken. I led him into his bedroom, cleaned and disinfected the wound, and plastered him up, only to discover that his foot was bleeding as well. Neither wound was serious, but I was almost as shaken as he was. As I was getting him into bed, he made a remark which was the nearest I ever heard him come to complaining.

"This business of being disabled sucks."

On a bad day he made the following remark. I didn't take that to be a grievance either. It was a statement anyone who had a throbbing headache may have made.

"I wish there was a pill I could take to make me sleep forever."

On another such day he said, "I want this to go away. I don't care how it goes away. I can also go away; that's fine."

I recall holding his hand and saying nothing, nothing at all. You learn not to say anything when a sick person makes a remark like that. There's nothing you can say, so you don't even try. Sometimes you open your mouth, intending to speak words of comfort, but you soon realise that since you yourself have not experienced that pain, you have no words of consolation. They don't exist in your mind, because your mind hasn't been there. So you simply squeeze his hand and after a little while, he squeezes yours, and you go to the pill box to get another painkiller.

On a better day, he was shuffling along, singing the shuffling song as usual.

I said, "Okay, tell you what—let's go play cards, I'll shuffle and you can deal. What game would you like to play?'

His swift reply was, "Fifty-two pick up."

"How do you play that?" I asked.

He chuckled, "I throw the whole pack up in the air and you pick them up!"

I know that's an old joke, but the way he said it was highly amusing.

Once, as I was leading him down the passage to the toilet, he was feeling guilty about putting me to so much trouble. He asked me what we were going to do when it got to the frail care stage. I told him we'd cross that bridge if and when we came to it. Then he laughed and said that would be the time to give him "the pill". Before I could say a word, he started singing the shuffling song and we laughed together.

Then there was the pastrami sandwich I offered him for lunch. He said it must be blessed and when I asked why, he jested, "Don't you see—Pastor Rami!"

I suggested that Pastor Rami must be an Indian preacher and he said,

"No, he's a military guy—Pastor Army!"

One could never get the last word in with Craig around, even in his enervating frame of mind.

One day I asked him, "What would you like to ask God for at this stage?"

"What do you mean?" he inquired.

"Well, do you still want God to heal you completely, or are you ready to go to Him, and simply ask that you go peacefully, without pain?"

"I can't answer that question," he said.

"Why?"

"Because that's is not my decision, it's God's."

I looked at him enquiringly. "But what if He gave you a choice?"

"Then I would ask for whatever He wants for me."

The day that Angela, the pastor's wife, came to visit was very funny. After Craig's fall, we allocated a special spot in the kitchen, where he would sit and smoke. We'd close the security gate, and he would hold on to the bars, enabling himself to sit in a chair that was placed in front of it. We'd light his cigarette for him, and he would blow the smoke out of the house. This was the scene when Angela arrived. She greeted him heartily.

"Oh dear," he said sheepishly, "I'm smoking in front of the pastor's wife!"

She laughed. "You have to do what you have to do," she said.

He contemplated for a moment, and then in a serious tone, asked her if she thought there were cigarettes in Heaven.

"Hmm," she replied, "I've never thought about that!"

With great hilarity, he declared that they probably had pearly ones up there!

Angela giggled. "Craig," she said, "I think it's time Pastor Gary and I came to pray for you again!"

It's delightful to have some joy in our lives from time to time. Craig makes joy. He makes it out of misery. *How does a person do that?* I ask. *How does he laugh when he's hurting?* If I ask him how he's feeling, he says, "Fine." I feel I should stop asking him, because it's not true; he's not fine. It makes me sad, but if he said he wasn't fine, I'd be even sadder. How silly is that? I have strange thoughts, thoughts that go round and round in my head, right thoughts, wrong thoughts, crazy thoughts, nonsensical thoughts; day and night. *I need some more joy; oh God, I need some more joy!* Then a good thought comes—*Craig brings joy—go talk to him.* So I do.

The time has come to get a hospice involved in our lives, another big step on this journey. I phoned Hospice East Rand (who I will simply refer to as Hospice from here on). I was told that we need the patient's permission before they could assist us, so we had the conversation with Craig. At first he couldn't justify a reason for engaging them.

"You and Dad are doing a great job," he told me, "We don't need anyone else."

I explained that they would visit weekly, and advise us on nursing techniques and administering the medication. He still didn't understand.

"You're doing fine," he insisted.

"Craig," I said in the kindest way I knew, "You won't be seeing the doctors again. A nurse from Hospice will come and assess you from time to time."

"Why? Can she make me live longer?"

Runaway time again. "No."

"So are you going to send me to Hospice then?"

"No my boy, we just need a bit of help and advice."

"Okay then, but it's for you and Dad, not for me."

"Right Craig, that's fine," I said, "It's for us."

Sister Debbie came to see us. I walked Craig through to the lounge to meet her and she had a long chat with him, asking him about his life before the tumour and indulging him in some pleasant conversation. I like her very much and have a good feeling about her. This is going to work well, but it won't be easy. Craig likes her too. She told me that Hospice assess terminal patients based on the symptoms they show towards the end of their lives. They can generally tell whether a person has months, weeks, or days to live, depending on their particular condition. I personally, have to adjust to many things; like the word "terminal". I hate that word; I hate it with a passion.

I told Sister Debbie that Craig had recently been suffering from nausea and vomiting and she suggested I get some anti-nausea tablets for him. Nausea is one of the symptoms of a brain tumour, but not one from which Craig suffered frequently. I subsequently visited my GP who gave me a script for the tablets. He said he'd be happy to issue scripts for any further medication that was requested by Hospice.

One day Georgie phoned to tell Craig she'd had to find another home for his dog, because she was going to live with her daughter, who lives in Alberton, near to where Craig's shop was. I walked into his room to find him sitting on his bed, sobbing inconsolably. Except for a few intermittent silent tears, that was the only time I ever saw him cry during his stay with us. I cannot describe my own grief. How I wished we could have taken Bam, but on the one occasion when Georgie dropped him off to spend the day with Craig, I had to separate him from our dogs and he barked at anyone—other than Craig—who came near him. He was a very aggressive little dog. Because of his memory loss, Craig forgot that incident, but the saddest thing was that some weeks later, he asked me what Georgie had done with the dogs. I had sworn I would never lie to him, but I was terrified to tell him, because I didn't want to face his grief all over again. Nevertheless, I told him. He looked sad, but was so ill by then, that he didn't have the energy to get upset. Mine was the heartache. He never asked again.

Monday, 5 March 2012

Sister Debbie comes once a week and has given me the names of a couple of caregivers who could assist if I need a break. At this stage I've been with Craig every day except Thursday, when I go to work and Ian stays with him. I get a break on Saturday afternoons, when Ian comes home from work, if I want to go anywhere, but I'm usually too tired by then, although I did go to a little get together at the quilt shop last Saturday. It was great to get out, because I haven't been there for months. Brian sat with his brother till Ian got home, but even though it was a pleasant afternoon, I couldn't stop thinking about Craig. His pain is there all the time, although we do control it with painkillers. One evening I couldn't get him to the bathroom, so Ian moved furniture around the house, turning our home somewhat upside down, but it doesn't matter. Georgie borrowed a wheelchair from a friend and she dropped it off here when she came to visit last month. We've put it in Craig's room, so the next step is to get him into it and wheel him to the loo. So far I haven't needed it, still managing to push or pull him around. His co-ordination is very bad and he can't balance, so it's quite an undertaking to steer him around. Even Ian can no longer take him outside because it's too much of an effort for Craig, so we let him smoke next to the open back door. At most, he smokes five cigarettes a day now. He sleeps most of the day, and only gets up to go to the loo, have a cigarette and hopefully eat a morsel of food. He can't get in and out of the bath alone, so Ian has to help him, but he does manage to wash and shave in the bath. I suppose it won't be long before someone has to bath him. I won't be able to deal with that, so will have to get help. We've already had some episodes with the toilet. It's awkward for both him and me, but a fear that we will both have to overcome, because he relies on help for almost everything he does. For him to brush his teeth, I leave the tap running, but he still can't put the toothbrush under the running water, and I have to help him get water to rinse his mouth out.

Cancer is a terrible, terrible thing. There are moments when I stand and look at my son lying there (he can't see me, because he's altogether blind now), and I picture the little boy he once was. I was recently paging through the album I made for him, with all his school reports, photos and bits and pieces that he made or acquired during his childhood and army days, then into his adulthood. There are so many memories that will never fade away. Craig was a shy little boy, who sailed through life trying to please everyone. In one of his kindergarten school reports, his teacher described him as "a dreamer, who is starting to wake up." The following year, the teacher called him "a quiet, well-mannered little boy who tends to be dreamy." She said his memory writing was very good—when he paid attention! Another teacher said he was "a quiet, hard-working little boy who tries hard to please." As he grew older, they said he wasn't day-dreaming so much. He never excelled at school, but he was a steady worker, and all his teachers remarked on how well behaved he was. I guess that's why he grew up to be called "Gentleman Craig" by the nurses in the hospital. After school, he was called up for national service in the South African Army, where he trained as a medic at a large military hospital. His letters home in those days are in his album, and I did some hearty chuckling as I read them this week. After the army, he completed a fitting and turning apprenticeship, and there he did excel, being the first South African student in twelve years to be awarded a distinction in Fitting and Machinery Trade Theory N2, for which he was awarded a floating trophy for best student. He subsequently went on to get distinctions in his N3, 4 and 5 exams, to qualify as a fitter and turner. Ironically, he hated this profession, and left his job after a couple of years, to pursue an entirely different vocation. Somewhere along the line he joined the National Sea Rescue Institute, doing volunteer work for the Fire Department. He had a few gruesome tales to tell about that. I look back now and wonder if we ever fully acknowledged his achievements. Maybe there's an odd sort of guilt which asks, *Were you good parents? Did you encourage him enough? Were you there for him at all times? Did you give him all the praise he deserved? Did you show him enough love? Where did you go wrong?* Of course we weren't perfect parents, and who of us can ever say we did everything right? When he went off the rails, was it our fault? No! We all make our own choices, and we all make wrong ones. Craig's life is summed up in his album, and I'm glad I have it, but it's not a necessary part of my memories. Right now I feel that his voice will continually ring in my ears, and I will feel his spiritual heartbeat. I will see his silhouette in the doorway of my own heart, and his laughter will echo in my thoughts, like distant bells that chime into the future. And a silent voice deep within that melody cries out, *My boy, my boy, you were not supposed to leave me!*

Tuesday, 6 March 2012

Time spent with my beloved son is precious. He will ask me ten times a day what time it is, followed by, "Day of the week?"

"Nine o'clock," I will reply, "And it's Thursday."

He knows that Martha comes on Thursdays, so he will mention that. Long term memory is one hundred per cent all right.

"Has Dad gone to work?"

"Yes."

Half an hour later, he will go through all the motions again, similar to dementia.

It's so sad, because he knows about his memory loss.

The conversation below is what we had today.

"I need to tell you what's happening in my brain."

"What?"

"It's telling me wrong things."

"Like?"

"That's why it's hard to push me around. Dad pushes me and my brain tells me that I'm falling over, so I feel as if I'm going to fall and I push backwards and then you tell me not to do that."

"I know Craig, but you're not falling over."

"You tell me that, but my brain is telling me that I'm toppling over, and I need to stop myself from falling, so I push backwards in order not to fall frontwards."

"I know Craig."

"Yes, but I need to tell you this, so you understand why I do that."

"We do understand Craig. We know your brain is telling you lies. Your brain is damaged my boy, and it's sending out wrong messages. That monster in your head is causing a lot of problems."

"I know. I only want to make sure you understand."

"We do."

And I really do understand. My own analogy is this:

You are about to sit on a chair, but you hear someone behind you pulling the chair away. The person tells you to sit down, but your brain tells you not to, because there is no chair there. So what do you do? Do you obey the person, or do you obey your brain? No matter how well you know the person, you have to listen to your brain, because you know you'll get hurt if you don't. So it is with Craig. What a dreadful situation this man is in! And what makes it worse is that he knows what's happening to him, but he can't control it.

Later

Craig used to tell jokes about a Zimbabwean fellow by the name of Lovemore Sibanda. We were fooling around, and I asked him about Lovemore.

In his best African accent, he replied, "Ah, Lovemore's got a cousin who works for Bakers Biscuits."

"Really?"

Referring to a particular type of biscuit, he quipped, "Yes, his name is Eet-Sum-Mor!"

The sad conversations often follow the amusing ones.

"Mom . . . ."

"Yes?"

"I'm not going to beat about the bush with this one."

"Then say it," I said.

"How long do you think?"

That gripped me. "I don't know. No one knows," I said.

"Well I can tell you it's not long. I need you to understand that."

"How do you know?"

No reply.

I took his hand. "Are you worried?"

"Only about you bunch."

"You don't need to worry about us. We have God. We'll be fine."

This was a tough one, because he knows very well we'll be devastated. It doesn't matter how much warning you have, how much pain you don't want him to have, how much preparation you try to make; you know you will still be gutted when the time comes. But I thank God for these conversations, because I doubt if anything will be left unsaid; nothing I can think of. It's my contention that if we have anything good to say to anyone, we should seize the moment, because we may never get another chance. A person doesn't have to be dying before we say, "I love you." A great blessing to me within this dreadful hardship is that I have so much opportunity to speak to my son from my heart. He doesn't want to be told I love him all day long. That would make him feel guilty about dying. He needs to feel loved by my actions, and I'm doing my best to make him feel good about that. I need to pay attention to him, even though some of his remarks are childish. He needs to be made to feel that his life is still worthwhile. I don't hide things from him. I answer his questions truthfully, even though this can be very painful. He's not a child and I cannot tell him I'm going to kiss the sore and make it all better.

"Are you scared?" I asked.

"No."

"Do you speak to God?"

"All the time."

"He won't necessarily answer your prayers the way you want you know, but He will answer them," I assured him. "You can ask Him anything at all."

He was thoughtful.

"Just ask Him Craig. Ask him whatever is on your heart."

"Okay."

I think we both know what he will ask.

Later—sitting by the back door, smoking.

"You should have been filming me since I came to live with you." (Last three months).

"Why?"

"So that people can see what happens when you have a brain tumour."

"What do you mean?"

"Well, think of all the things I could still do when I came to stay with you and look at me now."

"Why on earth would we want to film that?"

"So they can use it for research." He sniggered, "And you could make money out of it!"

I was shocked. "What? Do you think I would use your illness to make money?"

"Why not?" he said, smiling, "Might as well get some benefit out of it."

"Well I'm not making a film," I said, "But I am writing a book. You know that."

"Yes."

"If I was making a film, or writing a book, what would you say to the people about brain tumours?"

"I'd tell them smoking helps!"

"Craig!"

He reflected for a while and then added, "I'd tell them they need a strong family."

I gulped. "Do you have a strong family?"

"Yes."

"What else would you tell them?"

"Not to be afraid to take their pills. Can I go back to my room now?"

"Of course."

I took the remains of the cigarette from his hand, and, on my instruction, he pulled himself up on the bars of the security gate. I took hold of his hands, turned him around and walking backwards, led him to his bedroom. Another sleep was imminent.

Friday, 9 March 2012

Yesterday I had to go back to the hospital to get the monthly medication. I'd been dreading that. We've conquered such a lot there, yet a simple assignment like collecting medication, was virtually causing me to develop an ulcer. I think it was a psychological hang up on my part, because I'd never been there without Craig. I didn't want to be there without him, and yet I didn't want him to ever have to go there again. I wished he'd never been there in the first place; I wished he'd never had to. That place was full of memories that I wanted to blot out, never to be reminded of. I knew I had to get the medication, but I didn't want to go. If it was simple, if one could just go there, hand in the script and get it filled, I could have dealt with the idea, but I had no doubt in my mind this would not be the case. Nothing is ever simple at The Hospital.

My dear friend, Trudy, came to the rescue by offering to come with me. If I thought I'd experienced all the horrors of that institution, guess what? I was wrong! One of the painkillers is a schedule seven drug, and you have no idea what a performance it is to get your hands on it! Trudy and I were away from home for seven hours. Having my friend sitting in the pharmacy with me was a life saver, because I didn't have to mull over the jovial banter I used to have there with Craig. He'd either be ragging me about my crocheting, telling me I came from another era, or explaining the shortcomings in my driving skills. Those conversations make me cry now. As it was, I bumped into some patients we'd met over the years and it was good to see how they were getting on and to be able give them a big hug, but it did bring tears to my eyes. They were upset to hear about Craig, because he'd become part of their lives, in a strange sort of way. He'd sown some positivity into their hearts. He'd reached out to other survivors. In a place like that, you never knew if you were going to see your new friends again, and they sensed they wouldn't see Craig. Thousands of patients pass through there every day and yet at least ten people, including nurses, pharmacists, doctors and clerks, asked after Craig. They'd never seen me there without him and it was touching to know they remembered him. He had obviously made an impact on people.

Saturday, 10 March 2012—Email

Craig's health has been on the decline for the past few weeks. Ian and I have been working hand in hand to try and make him as comfortable as possible, but have accepted that he doesn't have long to live. The "intelligence" side of his brain is still intact, which essentially makes this even harder, because he knows exactly what's going on, and although I think it would probably be better if he didn't, it has allowed me to have some amazing talks with him. Sister Debbie has told me how blessed I am to be able to have this type of communication with my son. She says it's unusual for patients in this state of health to be open to speaking so freely about it. Having said that, I sometimes watch him lying there with his eyes wide open, seemingly staring at the ceiling, with the saddest look on his face and I can't help wondering what is going through his mind. Even though he's blind, he insists on putting on his glasses every time he gets out of bed. When I asked him why he does that, he says it makes him feel more comfortable. He's been wearing glasses since he was fifteen, so I can understand that. The only times he gets out of bed is to go to the toilet, and in the evenings, when he sits in the lounge with us for up to an hour, listening to the TV and having a bit of supper. He's eating significantly less, and has lost a lot of weight. Ian helps him to bath, but we are wondering how much longer he'll be able to do that. When Ian pushes him around, he shuffles along, because he can't lift his feet off the ground. The wheelchair helps, but the house isn't big, so it's easier to manoeuvre him about on his feet. I still hold his hands and pull him along as I walk backwards. He sits on the bed, but struggles to get into it, so we have to take him through the motions of which leg to lift, and when to turn. His left side, where the tumour is, is particularly bad. The worst thing is the headaches, which are ever there. We've been told to give him as many painkillers as he needs. I used to be paranoid about this, but it has become easier, because I don't want him to suffer. He has a high pain threshold, so doesn't require as much medication as one might think. I monitor the painkillers carefully; I even have my own little "nurse's chart" in his room.

A few weeks ago we were getting very little sleep because Craig was waking in the night, in terrible pain, but that's much better now and he sleeps well. I'll be interviewing a caregiver next week. At the moment I'm only working one day a week and since Ian has that day off work, he looks after Craig, so this is a full time job, but we manage well.

Wednesday, 14 March 2012

I had a bad night last night. I woke at 1:00 a.m. and that was the end of any shut-eye I hoped I might get. That's how it goes. Craig is the same today. He had his half glass of milk, toilet, cigarette and painkiller, and is now back in bed. He doesn't miss a trick on the radio though. I don't know what to think about that. His legs are so thin now; he isn't that big bloke from the ink shop any longer.

I spoke to Edith on the phone and she said my voice didn't sound good, but it may be just tiredness. I've been coughing a bit lately too, especially in the mornings, but yesterday I did my lung exercises and that helped. This ludicrous lung disorder of mine hasn't left me as I'd hoped it would, so I'll have to be careful. I can't afford to get sick now.

Saturday, 17 March 2012

Today Craig was listening to the radio when he informed me the song they were playing was really stupid. When I asked why, he said it was because the words went like this: "Whatever doesn't kill you will make you stronger." He then took the handful of pills that I gave him and sighed, "I wonder if these are going to kill me, because they are not making me stronger!" Good point.

Monday, 19 March 2012

The caregiver started with us today and I went to work, albeit with my heart in my mouth, but the day went well. Her name is Winnie. She's good with him. Doug, Brian and Debbie are taking care of her wages. We've agreed that she should come twice a week, one day of which I'll go to work, and the other day I can get a break to catch up on shopping, or whatever.

Chapter 20

Watching one's child die is horrific. My hope and faith for his recovery have been unremitting, but his quality of life is so poor now, that for his own sake I find that I can no longer pray for his healing. He has survived some hopeless situations and his life has been spared many times. He has beaten the odds concerning the given life span for a person with a glioblastoma multiforme brain tumour. The Internet says that some patients have been known to live for three years or longer and no one knows why. I believe that God set out the days of our lives before we were born, and although I know many folk get healed, I also know that some do not. I don't know why; only God does. That's why I told Him over three years ago, when I was desperately asking Him to heal my son, that no matter how this ended, I would never stop trusting Him, because He knows what's best for Craig. That doesn't mean that I have reservations about the healing power of Jesus Christ—not at all. The scripture that God gave me in 2008, which I mentioned earlier in this book, was "Trust in the Lord with all your heart (which I do) and lean not on your own understanding". So there's the key. We can never understand God's ways. We will never understand why some folk are healed and others are not, but He knows why, and I trust Him. I don't know why stuff happens, but I do believe there is a divine purpose behind it, a purpose which the human mind will never be able to comprehend. Some years ago, I came across one of the most profound quotations I have ever read. I would like to share it here:

> Be patient toward all that is unsolved in your heart and try to love the questions themselves, like locked rooms and like books that are written in a very foreign tongue.
> Do not seek the answers which cannot be given, because you would not be able to live them.
> And the point is, live everything. Live the questions now. Perhaps you will then, gradually, without noticing it, live along some distant day into the answer.
> *Rainer Maria Rilke*
> *From Letters to a Young Poet*
> *Letter No. 4, July 16th 1903.*

By grasping the meaning of this, I am able to get through each day of this traumatic time of my life, and believing that God Almighty has a perfect plan for my son, is my survival kit. I rest in the knowledge that because Craig has accepted Jesus Christ as his Lord and Saviour, he is going to a place where he will be with Him for eternity. That is one answer that I already have. The best thing is that Craig knows this too; he speaks openly about it. Humans are strange creatures though. I've often had to leave his room because my tears are choking me—my writing is far braver than my emotions. He's almost totally bedridden now; his co-ordination is erratic; he cannot walk and he eats hardly anything. Fortunately, the headaches are controllable. He sleeps most of the day and night, but is lucid when he's awake and still manages a little joke here and there, taking great delight in pulling my leg about my nursing abilities or whatever. He is the most incredible patient.

Wednesday, 21 March 2012

The past two days have been immensely trying. Getting this fellow to eat anything is unachievable. Favourite foods don't exist anymore. He's very frail and I'm not sure if it's because he's not eating, because of the medication, or because he gets no exercise whatsoever—probably a combination of all three. Today I battled to get him to the bathroom; I don't think I can continue to do this. I thought he was going to fall, so I began to pray. Craig didn't fall, but I think that may have been a warning. It must be time to get a commode. I'm finding the wheelchair too difficult to push from the bedroom to the toilet; there are too many tight corners. One time I could barely get him into the wheelchair, and then I couldn't get him out. I eventually overcame everything and got him back to bed. Ian and I are endeavouring to make him comfortable, but we end up with a feeling of helplessness. Mankind takes so much for granted, but ultimately our abilities are a matter of grace. It's such a shame that something like this has to happen before most of us realise that.

Craig is seriously ill and I hate to see him suffer, so if the Lord chooses to take him home, then I'm at peace with that, even though my grief is almost unbearable. Craig concedes that God can heal him, but right now I think he would rather be in Heaven with Jesus. There are days when I feel I can't go on, but I know I will. Last night I was feeling very down. I was sitting at my computer, and decided to send an email to Edith, because I'm able to share so much of this with her. I typed it out, but didn't send it, because I hate to revive her pain, even though she says she's okay with it. I've pulled the mail of my draft box, and decided to put it in this book. I want others to know that we're allowed to feel pain and to express it.

Hi my dear Friend
This is getting so hard now. Winnie's good (the caregiver). She detected that Craig may start getting bed sores because he's not moving—back and bum are red. She put him on his side, and has made a chart saying what time he's been turned. I've been writing up a chart for the painkillers for some time now, so the room is starting to look like a hospital ward, what with the medication etc. When Ian came home from work, Winnie told him to turn Craig regularly. He phoned to tell me just before I left the office, and I bawled the whole way home. The slightest thing is getting to me now; I guess it's a build-up. I feel I can't take much more. My heart is bleeding and bleeding and bleeding. But you know. Wish I could stop telling you, but I know you truly understand. I don't want to do anything. I don't want to go anywhere.
You and I are holding hands, as our kids will do.
Lotsa luv
Leonie

Sunday, 25 March 2012

A great friend of mine called Norma, in England, wrote and told me a beautiful story, which I will relate in her words:

A lady was out walking the dog in the countryside, and saw what looked like a little lamb all huddled up at the base of a tree. She climbed over the fence, and then over the barbed wire, and picked the little lamb up, and put it inside her coat. It was still alive, but only just. She knocked on the shepherd's door and he held out his arms to his little lamb, telling her not to worry, he would look after the little lamb, he would put it by the fire and then give him a bottle, and soon he would be out in the fields gambling along with all the other little lambs. The lady walked away with her coat

> all torn and dirty, but it didn't matter; she'd helped to rescue a little lamb, so went home rejoicing.

Norma asked me if my little lamb was in the hands of the Shepherd yet. What a tender way of expressing the love of Jesus! I told her he is. I am so blessed in that knowledge. Craig has no fear of dying because he knows exactly where he's going, and what a wonderful place it is.

We get to a point where we know there is no more we can do, except love and care for our little lambs. I am the lady with my coat all torn and dirty and I truly don't mind at all. What this story says to me is that I have helped to rescue this little lamb, and that I too shall rejoice. Craig loves the Lord and I pray for him each night before he goes to sleep. I ask him if he'd like me to read to him from the Bible, and he usually says yes. A while ago I told him to keep God's words in his heart, and not his head, because his brain is damaged and he won't remember what's in his head. I said he should keep peace in his heart. I'd ask him what was in his heart and he'd say, "Peace," which made me feel very good. One night I again asked him what was in his heart. He sighed and said, "Blood!" Oops! I don't know whether he was being funny, or whether he had forgotten about the peace, so the next night I repeated the question. His answer was "Love", and I decided that was all right too. At times he's very childlike, and then suddenly he will do a turnaround, reminding me that he is an adult, which means I also have to do a turnaround and treat him like one! This is so hard. He is an adult and yet he has become a child again.

Ian seems to think it can't be long now, but I'm not so sure. Our son is fragile and has lost a colossal amount of weight, but he's still fighting. I battle to move him around because he's tall and has big bones. He resists us when we hold him and try to move him forward, because his brain continues to tell him he's falling.

I've managed to visit a couple of churches over the last four weeks, while either Doug or Brian comes to sit with Craig. I encourage Ian to go to the flying field because he needs to wind down at least once a week. Today I visited the Baptist church down the road from where we live, and felt truly comfortable there. This is a difficult time to make a change, especially after eighteen years in one place, but in this church I feel more love and peace than I've felt in a long time. The pastor preached on blind Bartimaeus, and as we approach Easter, he wove the sermon into the message of the Cross. He spoke a lot about spiritual blindness, but related it to physical blindness—this was amazing, as the Lord reminded me of the scripture He gave me three and a half years ago concerning Craig. I quote it again:

> I will bring the blind by a way that they knew not; I will lead them in paths they have not known: I will make darkness light before them, and crooked things straight. These things will I do unto them, and not forsake them. (Isaiah 42:16) (KJV)

When first I read this scripture, I took it quite literally, believing that God would heal our son's blindness. My prayers were answered and Craig was able to see well enough to drive a car for a couple of years after that. When I look back on all the prayers that were answered, I stand in awe of our Great God, who is so much bigger than our problems. Craig has lived for three years longer than the life expectancy of a GBM patient, but now my prayers have changed and I know that Craig's have too. He doesn't want to live like this. I now see this verse as relating to a spiritual blindness, with a promise of light in eternity and a glorious hereafter. Craig was spiritually blind long before he was physically blind, but God showed him spiritual sight and he is looking forward to a future without any pain or sorrow.

Friday, 30 March 2012

Ian leaves for work at 5:45 a.m. each day, and after he left this morning, I lay awake in bed for about an hour. I cried and I felt Jesus holding out His hand to me. He is so gracious. I'm dreadfully emotional at the moment and can hardly write this. Using the commode has accentuated the gravity of Craig's sickness. My boy is so helpless. I want to scream as I write this. I want to scream and scream until I run out of voice. The craving for nicotine is still evident in his body, but he only smokes about three or four cigarettes a day now. Early this morning I allowed him to smoke in his room, and he had some coffee. I hold the cup and he drinks from a straw. He used the commode and didn't even seem to notice that he wasn't on the toilet in the bathroom. I had opened the windows wide for the smoking, and when he got back into bed I half shut them. He asked what I was doing, and he couldn't fathom why I had opened them, because he didn't realise that he'd smoked in the bedroom. For the last hour he's been lying on his back, eyes wide open, seemingly staring at the ceiling. Sometimes I think I see a tear in those eyes, but I'm not sure. I feel myself crying out, *How am I going to do this, Lord? How am I going to do this?*

Until recently, Ian was walking him to the bathroom and helping him into the bath. He could still wash himself, but we could see that this was becoming extremely stressful for him, and so we decided that now was the time for him to be bed bathed. This was yet another traumatic step for all of us. My daughter-in-law, Lindy, who was a nursing sister for twenty five years, came to bath him today. This was problematic for me, because she wants me to learn to do it, but I'm not ready to face bathing my forty year old son. Again, I cry, *I didn't want this!* Winnie is a compassionate caregiver, dedicated to helping Craig. She will bath him twice a week and somehow we will have to manage in between, although I know Lindy will come again if needs be. Craig was so grateful that he didn't have to go to the bathroom that he had no objection to being bathed by his sister-in-law. In fact, I don't think he'd have had any objection anyway. He's oblivious to many things. He's so ill, it doesn't bother him anymore.

I've learned a lot about this complex member of our bodies called "The Brain". In Craig's case, his short term memory has been badly affected, but he's aware of the past and the present. It's become obvious that he places no value on material things. Not that he was ever materialistic, but now he knows only the value of life itself, and even that he is slowly letting go of. His muscles and nervous system are weak, his eyes are blind. He gets shaky from time to time, and his co-ordination has become a lot worse than it was even a few weeks ago. In one of his more clear-headed moments, I told him how proud his Dad and I are of him for the way he has dealt with his disability. He modestly told me that we were the ones who had handled it well. Even though he sleeps a lot, he's quite hard work when he's awake. He's very much aware of what Ian and I are doing for him. We deal with it differently, but we manage to pull together. They say men are from Mars and women from Venus, and I can relate to that. Even our ways of dealing with our emotions are not similar, yet I sense that throughout the battle of the past four months, we have been drawn closer to one another than we have ever been. A situation like this can either make or break you, to coin a phrase. In our case, through the grace of God, it is making us. It doesn't happen automatically, and it isn't easy. In fact, it's the hardest thing we've ever had to do.

Our time of mourning has already started. We're mourning the way our son used to be; we're mourning the life he once had. To see him now is tragic. It feels like a bad dream, frenetic, and unstoppable. It's overcast today and very, very quiet. I feel as though I'm floating in some unknown place, knowing that my feet will never touch the ground, because I have no feet. What a strange sensation. I wonder what sort of sensations Craig has. The other day he told me that the headaches were only temporary. That's his gentle way of telling me that he's nearing the end of his life. As I write, I'm looking at photos of him, smiling and laughing in happy days. He and I both know there will be happy days again, happy days forever.

Monday, 2 April 2012

What a terrible day I had at the hospital, totalling nine hours, excluding travelling time. Is there anything other than a terrible day in that place? They wouldn't give me the medicine because they claimed Craig had an outstanding account. I wanted to spit blood. I'd been told that was sorted out. When he was initially admitted in 2008, forms had to be filled in with all his details, including his monthly income. The Hospital does charge patients who have an income, according to what it is. Therefore, at the outset, they would have charged for his treatment, albeit not a large amount. After his first operation, he quit the job he had because he was no longer able to do it. At that stage, he should have notified them of his change of income, but he wasn't aware of that. Had he done it, his status would have been downgraded, and he would have been charged a lesser amount, according to his current income, if any. It was only when he applied for admission to hospital for his third operation, that he was informed that he owed seventeen thousand rand, and what was he going to do about it? Craig declared that he had never received a statement of account from them and was not aware that he owed money. The short version of this story was that I managed to establish that he would have to discuss the matter with the accounts department, so we went to see them, and they referred us to a lady who they said would be able to "make a plan". They couldn't refuse him admittance for surgery, but they insisted that we made some agreement concerning the unsettled amount. The lady we saw was extremely helpful, asking Craig to submit proof that he was now no longer employed. We explained to her that he had owned a shop for two years, but had paid himself a minimal salary and had since handed over the shop to a new owner, free of charge. The lady said all he had to do was provide proof of this and supply his bank statements for the past three months, and there would be no further charge from The Hospital. Craig explained that he had absolutely no assets, because when he was told he was dying, he had given everything he owned to his partner and was now penniless. Therefore, he was unable to pay any outstanding amounts. Both Craig and I were given to understand that the old account would be written off. Hmph!

Now, whilst my son was lying in bed at home terminally ill, I was told I would once again have to go to the accounts department and "sort this out." I was pleased that Trudy had accompanied me again, because my own mental capacity could carry me no further. It felt like we were walking nine hundred miles to the accounts department. Certainly, it was the longest walk I've ever done in that ghastly place. Once there, queues were not the difficulty we faced, but yet a new form of adversity. I hardly remember what I said to the people there, but I do know that one person told me to stop being so negative when I mentioned that my son was dying. I asked them if they felt that I was responsible for my forty year old son's debt, to which they retorted that I was not, but since he was receiving a Government disability grant, he would have to use that. I undertook to explain that said grant didn't anywhere near cover the costs incurred at this point in time, but my pleading fell on deaf ears. They were relentless, and in the end I was coerced into signing an agreement to say I would pay the seventeen thousand rand in instalments, before they would let me take possession of the medication. Ian and I cannot afford over a thousand rand per month for the medication, so I will have to continue collecting it from The Hospital on a monthly basis. The government provides it free of charge under Craig's circumstances, but what a performance to get it. On Trudy's wise advice, I included a hand-written clause, stating that I would no longer be responsible for the debt after Craig passed away. By the time we left, hours after waiting in the pharmacy for the medication, I had a burning pain in my chest. Ian had to go to a meeting at 6:00 p.m., but fortunately I arrived home in time to take care of Craig.

He's a handful tonight, which is tough after a day like I've had. I was so worried that I'd signed my life away that I phoned Doug asking for assurance that I wouldn't end up in jail! He convinced me I'd be able to live the rest of my life free of a criminal record. *How much more?* I ask, *How much more?*

Friday, 6 April 2012

Craig asked me, as is common a few times each day, what day of the week it was, so I told him it was Friday, Good Friday in fact. He assured me he knew what that meant, and I went on to remind him of the story of the crucifixion, and that because Jesus suffered and died on that cross to atone for our sins, we now have the promise of eternal life in Heaven with Him.

"All we have to do is believe in Him," I said.

Craig nodded in agreement and asked me, "So, can I go there now?"

My silence must have burned his ears, so he added, "I'm so tired of these headaches Mom."

I struggled to say, "Have you asked Him, Craig? Why not ask Him?"

He looked at me with those big blind eyes and said, "The Bible says I can ask anything in His Name and He will do it."

"Yes," I said quietly, "If it's His will, He'll do it."

Sunday, 8 April 2012

Conversation with my extraordinary son tonight:

"Debbie phoned—not Sister Debbie, but Debbie your sister."

He grinned.

"I spoke to her partner Simon too. He's been praying for you."

"Say thanks," Craig said, "And tell him I'll pray for him as well. If he's going to be part of this family, then he will need it!"

Oh my! I think he will die with his sense of humour still intact. He makes the most unlikely remarks.

Chapter 21

An Israeli business colleague of Doug's told him he was going to the Old City of Jerusalem at Passover, and asked if we would we like him to place a prayer in a crevice of the Wailing Wall. What a kind gesture that was, coming from a Jew who knows we are Christians. I wrote the prayer, most of which was taken from the Bible. I have pondered about whether to print it in this book, but have decided to do so, because it is my view that this type of supplication can be placed before the Father by those who are losing loved ones, and are no longer able to pray for the healing of their earthly bodies. My relationship with God is what kept me going as I walked this incomprehensible road with my son, and I believe it is His desire to help others in the same way.

> Hear, O Lord, our righteous plea; listen to our cry. Give ear to our prayer—it does not rise from deceitful lips. We call on you, O God, for you will answer us, give ear to us and hear our prayer. Show the wonder of your great love, you who save by your right hand those who take refuge in you from their foes.
>
> Keep Craig as the apple of your eye; hide him in the shadow of your wings. He has set the Lord always before him. Because you are at his right hand, he will not be shaken. Therefore his heart is glad and his tongue rejoices; his body will also rest secure because

> you will not abandon him to the grave. You have made known to him the path of life; may you fill him with joy in your presence, with eternal pleasures at your right hand. And even though he walks through the valley of the shadow of death, may he fear no evil, for you are with him, your rod and your staff they comfort him. Surely goodness and love will follow him all the days of his life and he will dwell in the house of the Lord forever.
> Heavenly Father, may the peace of God, which transcends all understanding, guard Craig's heart and his mind in Christ Jesus, for the rest of his days on this earth. And Craig—in righteousness, shall see your face.

Below is an email that Doug later received from his Jewish friend:

> My pleasure Doug. I'll be heading to the Old City of Jerusalem later today. I'll print your prayer and place it in a crevice of the 2,000+ year old walls that surrounded the temple mount, traditionally, the holiest place on earth. I pray along with you, that all be well with your brother.

How blessed is that! After placing the prayer in the crevice, he sent photos he had taken of the Wailing Wall and the Old City walls.

Wednesday, 11 April 2012

I've attended a local Methodist church a few times, and this morning the minister came to our house to take Holy Communion with Craig. It was a blessed experience, attended my myself and Winnie. It's gratifying to know that Craig is at peace with the Lord. I've had plenty of time to speak to him about spiritual matters, to pray with him, and to read passages of Scripture to him. A year or so ago I bought him a Bible with large print because of his failing eyesight. He can't read it now, but it stays on his bedside table and he enjoys hearing God's Word during his lucid moments. One day, about six weeks ago, I recited Psalm 23 to him. I've heard him recite it himself, so I suggested he do it. After a few lines, he got stuck, so I asked him to repeat each line after me. As we neared the end, he followed my lead—"Surely goodness and mercy . . . will follow me all the days of my life . . . And I will dwell in the house of the Lord . . . forever." My next words were, "See, there you go!" and grinning, he repeated, "See, there you go!" Nothing wrong with that side of his brain! There are undeniably joyous moments. We're living them together, every moment.

Tuesday, 17 April 2012

Our boy is slowly slipping away. He talks very little, although he can still muster a smile for the odd visitor. On Good Friday I went to the Methodist church and to the Baptist church on Easter Sunday. I love them both. Good Friday was an emotional service for me, hence my decision to join the Baptists on Easter Sunday, because I thought their service would be a little less of a tear jerker. Oh my word! I bawled all the way home! What an amazing account of the Resurrection and what lies in store for my son.

Friday, 20 April 2012

Things are tough, very tough indeed. I think we'll soon be asking Winnie to come in more than her present two days a week. Ian and I manage together, but he works a five day week, so I'm with Craig more than he is. We are blessed to have three other tremendous kids, who, along with their respective spouses, are supporting us both emotionally and financially as they walk alongside their beloved brother.

Monday, 23 April, 2012

Since Craig became ill, we've made some wonderful friends overseas, friends whom we may never meet face to face, but who faithfully write emails of encouragement to us as a family. I cannot recount all the messages we've had, but have chosen one to share in this chapter. There have been many others, each one as special as the one we received this week from a lady called Gill, in Australia:

> Even though we have never met, I feel like you are a dear friend having little chats to me about what you are going through. You write from your heart, all your hopes and trials over the years, as you have watched an amazing son fight this valiant battle. You may not feel like it in your downtimes, but you have been a mighty witness of the Lord's ever loving arms around your family, you have kept your eyes on Him, the author and perfector of your faith.
>
> These days are oh so precious as you watch Craig's earthly battle draw to an end, to the time that he will be welcomed into his eternal home with the words "Welcome home, thou good and faithful servant". He will dwell in a place that there will never be another tear (one of my favourite verses from Rev. 7:17)—oh! What a promise in this tear soaked world.
>
> May the risen, conquering Lord Jesus wrap His loving arms around you now as a family—may His presence be very real to you all. We will continue to uphold you in prayer—upheld before the Throne of God—what better place to be?

Sunday, 29 April 2012—extract from my journal

I wonder how many seasonal changes I've watched through the big glass windows of our sun lounge. On 3 September last year I wrote that spring was here. That was eight months ago, and now the autumn season is almost over, as we go into winter, and surely a winter of our lives. Most of the leaves have fallen off that big tree and we can clearly see the birds. It's a sunny day, as if someone is trying to tell us that all will be well.

Friday, 4 May 2012

Today was "collect Craig's medication from the hospital day." I still can't bring myself to go alone, so my brother, Tony, came with me. He was shocked by the goings on there. We had to go to the clinic to get a script for the schedule seven painkillers, and there we had a nasty encounter with a patient who assumed we were jumping the queue. He was waiting for a consultation, whilst we were waiting for a script, so we weren't jumping the queue, but tensions become high when people wait hours, and they get rather restless at times. The man was yelling at me, leaving me no gap for explanation, so by the time we left, I was a nervous wreck, and I think Tony was ready to walk the plank. I was grateful that he was there though. Without moral support, I think I'd have collapsed. My son was dying, and someone was shouting at me for attempting to get his medicine. Where's the sense in any of this?

As we were leaving, I was allowing myself to believe that no good thing could come out of a visit to The Hospital, when I spotted Tanya, the lady whose eye had to be removed because of a tumour. She and her husband recognised me immediately, instantly noting the absence of Craig. I had to tell them that he wouldn't be going there again, because he was deemed to be dying. Oh, the sadness on their faces. Tanya knew what he had been through; she understood. And yet, through her sadness, I could be happy. Her surgery had been successful. She only had one eye now, but as far as she knew, the tumour had been eliminated.

Sunday, 6 May 2012

I'd like to share the discussion I had with my boy today. I guess I will always call him my boy. He's not a boy, but he's *my* boy. His short term memory is worsening, although he remembers his past in detail, and whatever is happening at the present moment. Added to that, he can hold sensible discussions, which although short, are quite normal. Today he agreed that I should read to him. I sat in his room and began to read passages from his Bible. He listened attentively for much longer than he is normally able to do, and God revealed to me a tiny portion of the spiritual level which Craig is now approaching. It's a place which none of us could ever fully comprehend and which I cannot even explain. My Holy Saviour has given me such peace in the midst of this tumultuous storm.

When I stopped reading, Craig started mumbling, but I couldn't hear what he was saying, so I asked, "Do you understand what I've been reading?" and his answer was, "I said, Amen, didn't I?"

I went on to speak to him about Heaven and who I thought he was going to meet there, and he seemed to be at complete peace with that idea. Then his hand moved around the bed, searching for something which he said he couldn't find.

When I asked what he was looking for, he said. "I don't know. I had something in my hand; I think it was a Bible or something."

I put the Bible into his hand and said, "There you go, is this what you were looking for?"

"Yes," he answered, "But you had best put it away safely now." Then he tilted his head and fell asleep. He looks like a baby when he's sleeping, not a forty year old man who used to do all the things other men do. I have to remind myself he's a man. He's the bravest man I've ever known.

Monday, 14 May 2012

The word "hallucination" fascinates me, because I don't see Craig's visions as such. They are incredibly real to him. He often sees strange people and signboards displaying well-defined words, such as "School" and "Everest". I question him about these signs, but have not been able to ascertain their meaning. Once he saw crowds of strangers, rushing about, and he was frustrated because he couldn't identify them. He doesn't seem to be frightened by his visions, which I perceive to be dreams of a kind, with Craig reaching out to touch objects that aren't there. Or are they? Once he was convinced he could see a green blanket. Colours are prominent in his mind. Another time, he was convinced he was in a hospital. He described the ward in detail, but when I came to give him his medication, he was disturbed, because he said the neurosurgeons had taken all his medicine, and the bottle was empty. I put the pills in his hand, but he assured me they were the wrong ones. I had to leave the room and return later with his pills, by which time, of course, he had no recollection of the former incident. He told me there was a sign on the floor, but he couldn't see the writing because it was hidden behind the bed. When I asked if he could see me, he assured me that he could. He said my jacket was brown. My jacket was in fact, black. I'm certain the reason his blindness doesn't bother him is that he imagines he can see. In other words, he doesn't know he's blind. It's mind-boggling.

An element of incontinence has started, and challenge 999 was buying adult nappies. I'd hoped that I would never have to look upon the nakedness of my adult son, let alone to clean him up, but I'm afraid this has been impossible. I'd half expected it, but I don't think I would ever have been prepared for it, no matter how hard I tried. When Winnie isn't here, Ian and I do it. I was not born to be a nurse, but I got thrown in the deep end, and now I have to swim against a back-current of emotional distress. Just when you think you've overcome your fears, you find yourself falling down a manhole, at the bottom of which a man-eating monster lies in wait. My mind screams, *I want my son back! I want my son back, the way he used to be! Please, please give my son back!* And then my husband and I go to bed and sleep evades us.

Chapter 22

Some of the things Craig has said to me over the past few months have torn my heart apart. There have been times when my only answer was to hold his hand a little tighter than usual. Once when I was walking past his room, he called out to me in a desperate tone of voice.

I hurried in to witness a terrified look on his face.

"What is it, Craig?" I asked.

"I can't see! I can't see! Why can't I see?" he cried.

Oh my God, I thought. *He's only just realised he's blind!* I'd often told people he didn't know he was blind, and they couldn't understand how he could not know, but it was because he was having visions and he thought he could see, which, in an odd way, was comforting for everyone else. This day, his mind was clear, but his eyesight was not.

I sat down on the bed, stroking his cheek. "Craigie boy, you're blind. You have been for some time. It's because of the tumour."

In absolute bewilderment, he asked, "But what are they doing about it?"

"About what, my boy?"

"The tumour. What are the doctors going to do about it?"

I prayed for an answer.

"There . . . there's no more they can do. I . . . I'm so sorry."

"But they can't just leave me!" he cried.

Oh God, get me out of here! my thoughts bellowed. *This is my child! What mother can bear to tell her child there's nothing she can do for him? Get me out of here!*

"I'm sorry, Craigie. I'm so sorry," I murmured.

He turned his head and a tear fell onto his pillow.

"Can I please have a cigarette?" he said.

"Course you can."

He soon forgot the conversation, and as far as I know, he never worried about his blindness again.

I've come to regard Winnie as my friend. Friends don't have to stand on ceremony. On days when I'm not working, I mosey around in my dressing gown in the mornings before she arrives, waiting for the gate bell to ring, announcing her arrival. It doesn't matter if I look like something the cat dragged in. She goes in to greet her patient, who always greets her with enthusiasm. Then, depending on his immediate requirements, she will go into the kitchen to make coffee and toast for herself. I, in the meantime, will doubtless be toasting one of my addictive raisin buns, and making my cup of boringly black, sugarless tea. We sit down in the sun lounge together, and I will update her on any pertinent events of the night before. We often deliberate over Craig's status, and she tells me about other patients she has nursed over the years. I'm particularly interested in Wayne, who was in his forties when he died of cancer last year. There are days when I go out and days when I stay home, but Winnie and I never get under each other's skin. She knows her place, and whilst she's in my home with Craig, I know mine. Martha comes twice a week and the two of them get on well. When Ian comes home in the afternoons, he usually takes Winnie to the taxi rank to get her lift home. You could say she's one of us now, and I hope that one day, when all this is over, we'll be able to meet from time to time. It would be sad to think that after caring for our son, she might simply disappear from our lives.

In May, Winnie took a couple of weekends off, and a nurse called Helen came to look after Craig. The first time she came, there was a bit of a crisis, but she handled it well. I had learned very quickly that when patients are bedridden, all sorts of things can go wrong. Bed sores can develop, (although in Craig's case, they never did), unused limbs and muscles ache, and constipation is common, to name some of them. Although Craig was hardly eating, his body still had to get rid of the waste, but his bowels weren't working. Sister Debbie was worried that he might develop a 'plug', which could cause severe problems and pain, so a laxative suppository had to be administered. Helen did that and she had to deal with the consequences, but I suppose for her, it was all in a day's work. I'd already started to realise that this type of thing could occur when the caregiver was not on duty. Craig seemed none the wiser to what had taken place, which was a blessing. He was perfectly comfortable with Helen, as he was with everyone. The second time she came, she told me that Craig had told her all about his medical training at 1 Military Hospital, over twenty years ago. Helen was amazed at the detail he recalled, considering how forgetful he was about the present.

"It's like Alzheimer's," she said, and I agreed.

"He likes chatting," she observed.

"Yes," I replied sadly, "There's not much else he can do."

Towards the end of May, Georgie and her sister came to visit Craig. Winnie had him sitting in the chair when they arrived and he was able to chat to them for half an hour, but once they left, he could not recall that they were there.

Wednesday, 23 May 2012

A little cold that started in me a few days ago has gone to my chest and I'm coughing like a chug train. This chest of mine is such a nuisance. My doctor says he doesn't think it's contagious—just my on-going lung disorder. So now I'm on antibiotics and all the paraphernalia that goes with this bane of my existence. Count your blessings, that's what I say, count your blessings!

Friday, 25 May 2012

It's a beautiful May morning. Winter has arrived, yet the sun is shining and the birds are splashing away in the bird bath. Presently my boy is sitting back in a chair to try and get his circulation flowing—he gets very sore lying in the bed day and night, so we try to get him up for a couple of hours day. Winnie has a knack of lifting him out of the bed and manoeuvring him into the chair. He was joking with me a little this morning, which shows that he still has his wits about him, although he forgets what has been said almost immediately. He can hold a short, but intelligent conversation and, by the sounds, one would think there was nothing wrong with him, but once the subject is changed, he has forgotten the first conversation. Thus I continue to learn more about the human brain. Our son seems still to be fighting this disease. At one time I thought he was letting go, but his staying power is astonishing. A little over two months ago, when he was more rational, he told me that he didn't think it would be long, and yet now I don't think he realises he's dying. The brain is indeed an intricate work of genius and only its Creator could possibly know what's going on inside it.

This week the editor of the local hospice bi-annual newsletter was here to do a story on Craig's struggle with brain cancer. Today she phoned to ask if she could take photos of Craig and me. I had mixed emotions about this, because I don't want to remember my son as he is now, hence the photograph I have positioned above the TV, enabling me to see him every day as he used to be, happy faced and full of life. I was told the hospice photos wouldn't necessarily be published, and I made the decision to let her go ahead and take them. Craig was quite receptive to the idea, and when the lady thanked him for allowing her to take them, he astounded me once again by telling her she was welcome because if he could be of any help to others who may be suffering from a similar problem, then it was his pleasure. Despite his ordeal, he would still like to know that his infirmity could be of some value to others. How could I refuse to allow the publication after he'd given his own consent so willingly? What a legacy to leave to the world! The hospice newsletter is a worthy publication and I was humbled that my son and I could be a part of it.

The photo that the hospice published

Later the same day

At about 6:30 p.m. this evening, Craig had a seizure that lasted a few minutes. He called and said he was very cold, so I loaded him with blankets, even though it wasn't particularly cold. He began to shiver rigorously, grumbling about a dreadful smell in the room. I confess I did panic a little and frantically called for Ian. I thought our son was leaving us. He was visibly distressed, so I began to fervently pray, trying to convince him that there was no cause for concern, as I held back bucket loads of tears. I was holding on to Ian with one arm and leaning over Craig with my other hand on his chest. I think it was a minute or two before we realised that he was actually having a seizure. *Oh my Lord*, I thought, *I wasn't expecting this! The medication should be preventing it. This wasn't supposed to happen!* Of course, there is no "supposed to", or "not supposed to happen". One cannot assume or discount any possibilities. The tumour must be so large by now that chaos in some form is inevitable. Having said that, one of the neurosurgeons once told me that the size of a tumour is not necessarily what determines how dangerous it is. GBMs are very invasive, and the particular area of the brain under attack is the critical factor. A patient can die without warning, the minute the tumour penetrates a vital spot. Small tumours have been known to kill in a very short space of time. The big question is, "What is that tumour doing inside Craig's head?" It's a very frightening thought.

When he again asked, "Can't you smell that terrible smell?" I suddenly recalled that this was indicative of a brain tumour seizure, as is a bad taste. I told him I could smell it too, and that it would soon disappear. After he had calmed down, I came to the realisation that this could be an occurrence we would have to learn to accept from now onwards.

He was still feeling cold. Trembling, I gave way to my inner fear by asking Ian to take down the crocheted blanket. With my heart in an unknown dimension, and my eyes clouded over with salty liquid, I spread the blanket over my boy.

"Remember the blanket I was making for you?" I asked, "Remember how you used to gripe at me whenever I started knitting in the hospital pharmacy, while we were waiting for your medication?"

"Yup."

"You used to moan because you said I was rocking the whole line of seats in the waiting room."

"Mmmmm . . ."

"Well, here's your blanket, all finished. It looks great on your bed. Here, feel it against your face."

This was the second time I'd given him the blanket, but he'd forgotten that.

His blind eyes gazed into space. "Is that the crocheted blanket?"

"That's the one," I managed to say.

"Has it got all those colours?"

"Yes, Craigie, dozens of colours."

He lowered his chin to feel it. "Thanks, Ma," he said, "Thanks."

If he still has the blanket over him by the morning, I will have to explain it all again. I'm not sure I can do that, so I think I'll put it away again before I go to bed tonight. He'll have warmed up by then.

Saturday, 26 May 2012 (the next day)

I was right when I said he hadn't stopped fighting. I told him yet again that he was outstandingly brave.

"I've only done what anyone would do," he responded.

"You've been stronger than most," I told him. "Many people would have given up long ago."

"You have to tell them to go down fighting," he said.

"Are you still fighting?"

"Yes."

"You don't have to, you know," I said quietly.

There was no reply.

Sunday, 27 May 2012

Tonight I opened Craig's Bible at 1 John, Chapter 2 and the second half of verse 14. Why am I so surprised when words jump off the page at me? Last night Craig indicated that he was still fighting. Here's what I read to him tonight:

> I write to you, young men, because you are strong, and the word of God lives in you, and you have overcome the evil one. (NIV)

"God is writing to you, young man," I told him, "because you are strong in your faith. But do you understand what the Word of God is, Craig?"

His eyes portrayed his spiritual understanding of what I was telling him. So many times before his brain became so befuddled, I used to tell him to bury the words I was reading in his heart, and not his head, because his brain would not be able to retain them.

I continued, "In the Gospel of John, the Bible tells us that in the beginning was the Word, and the Word was with God and the

Word was God. It goes on to say that the Word became flesh, and made His dwelling among us. That means, Craig, that the *Word* was *God*, and He became flesh, and came to earth, in the form of His Son, Jesus. Do you understand that?"

A silent nod.

I read the verse to him again, ". . . and the Word of God lives in you . . . that means Jesus lives in you."

His blind stare emerged again.

I took his hand. "Craig, you know that God didn't cause this evil tumour?"

Of course he knows.

"God cannot cause evil. That came from the devil. Nobody knows why God didn't take it away, but He's telling you that your faith is strong, and that Jesus lives in you, which means you're going to Heaven."

He squeezed my hand.

"And you have overcome the evil one. That's the devil, Craig, you've beaten him. Now tell me, if you beat someone in a fight, do you carry on fighting?"

"No."

Oh, Lord, my heart cried out, *he's hearing me!*

"Of course you don't. You, my boy, have won this battle! You don't need to fight anymore. You're going to Heaven, where the devil cannot go!"

I could hardly believe my ears when Craig said, "Praise the Lord! Can I go to sleep now?"

God had put a smile on my face once again.

Wednesday, 30 May 2012

Winnie's been ill this week. She wasn't able to find a replacement at short notice, so I'm battling along on my own. I've been presented with some heavy challenges, which have made me rather touchy. Neurotic, maybe that's the word. Even though we are using nappies as a precautionary measure, Ian usually lifts Craig onto the commode. I don't have the strength to get him out of the bed, so I tried a bottle and a bucket, and nearly went off my rocker in the process. The emotional stress, coupled with the physical strain propelled me so close to the edge that I phoned Sister Debbie and asked her to pop by and help me. Fortunately she was available, and I managed for the rest of the day until Ian came home. Craig handled the whole thing better than I did. I asked Sister Debbie about the viability of a catheter. She told me that Hospice does not advocate catheters for terminally ill patients, because they don't know how long the patients will live, and infection can set in if they are used for too long.

Lindy however, has apparently come up with the answer to our problems—a mock catheter, which is a condom attached to a tube, with a urine bag at the other end. I'll get it from her tomorrow—challenge number 1000!

My saving grace at the end of a day is to sit and read to Craig. What solace I find in God's Word, and I believe he does too. Tonight I was joking with him about looking after my belongings in Heaven until I get there, and he said yes, he would. In fun, I've been telling people for years that I've ordered a cottage with roses in Heaven. I said Craig could stay there for the time being, but would have to move out when I arrived!

Hospice advises families to tell their dying loved ones that it's okay for them to go. Terminal patients need to know that their families are able to deal with them leaving. This evening I told

Craig we'd be glad to know that he was in Heaven, and not suffering here. Phew, phew, phew!

Last time we turned him onto his other side (7:00 p.m.), I told him he looked nice because his Dad had given him a shave. He knitted his brow and asked what time he'd had the shave. I told him 5:00 p.m., and asked him why he wanted to know.

"Because I'm trying to get things right in my head," was his reply.

It must be so difficult to try and arrange one's thoughts. I told him it wasn't important.

"You know you forget things, don't you?" I asked.

"Yes," he said, so I told him not to worry about it, because we would remind him. Phew, phew, phew again!

Friday, 1 June 2012

Today was another very demanding day. Winnie's still got the flu, but says she'll be back on Monday. Lindy brought the catheter contraption, and Ian and I set it up before he left for work this morning. It does work, but I have my doubts about how well. We shall see. I'm very stressed by all this. My son's got a brain tumour—I wasn't anticipating incontinence, and certainly not of this calibre. This is so horrible!

This morning Craig wanted to get up and go to work. I explained to him that he was ill and had to stay in bed. He became agitated, wanting to know who was looking after his shop. I told him someone was there and there was no need for concern. He seemed to accept that.

Saturday, 2 June 2012

He's in deep thought.

"What you thinking about?" I ask.

"The price of eggs."

"That's not funny!" I say, laughing.

He is silent, not a murmur.

Then I tell him, "You are supposed to laugh."

"But you told me it's not funny!"

It's at times like these when his brain disorder astounds me. There's no short term memory, yet he can easily respond to normal dialogue, even to the point of making jokes about it. I take his Bible, and read a few passages, followed by quite a long prayer, longer than usual—I'm not sure why; I just feel lead to do that. Then he asks for a painkiller and blindly focuses on my face. I know he can't see, yet he stares into my eyes, as though he can *think* with his eyes. I wave my hand in front of those big eyes, to make sure he can't see, even though I know he can't. Odd. Why do I do that? I pop the painkiller in his mouth and hold the glass of water to his lips. He swallows, seemingly with difficulty. My heart cries out, *Oh God! Oh God! Oh God!*

"Has the pill gone?" I ask.

"Gone where?"

And my heart cries out again. This is common discourse that we have. I will have to re-word the question.

"Is there anything in your mouth?" I ask.

"Yes."

"What is it?"

"A tablet," he answers.

I give him some more water. "Swallow the tablet, Craig,"

He swallows.

"Is there anything in your mouth now?"

"No."

"Well done," I say, "Now you can go to sleep."

"Thanks Ma," he says in such a tone that one would never know there was anything wrong with him. His eyes are still open, but he's asleep—so quickly.

"Sleep tight, my boy," I whisper, and I leave the room, blubbing.

Sunday, 3 June 2012

Nicky ran the Comrades in Durban today, completing the run within the specified time limit. This was her first attempt at the annual South African marathon, so was a great achievement for her. We told Craig about it a number of times, but he kept forgetting. When I spoke to her, I handed the phone to him. He congratulated her enthusiastically, telling her that next year she must run for him. I don't know if he thought he'd still be with us this time next year. I can't ask him questions like that.

Chapter 23

There's been chocolate in the house for the past two days, and I haven't eaten it. That's a statement.

We don't use the catheter in the daytime, because it's not entirely successful, but it does serve a purpose at night. The nappies aren't enough, and Ian and I have repeatedly had to change the bed linen and Craig's clothes in the middle of the night. The problem is that the condom tends to slip off, but when it doesn't, it helps.

A few months ago, we were given some reading material by Hospice, providing sound, yet empathetic advice on how to cope with our own emotions and those of our loved ones, as well as their physical needs when they are dying. It wasn't easy reading, but very helpful for families who are enduring the trauma that sadly will come to many at some stage of their lives. Hospice people know what they're talking about; their input in Craig's life, and ours, has been invaluable. I have a coping mechanism of my own. It's called laughter; but lately there hasn't been much of that. I have to remind myself that somewhere within the depths of all the pain, there's something to be grateful for, something to smile about. Craig's problems are larger than life. He has no quality of life. He's nearing the end of his life. If anyone has anything to moan about, he does, but no grievance comes forth from his mouth. On the contrary, he makes me smile. He will say things which, intentionally or unintentionally, make me smile. If it's appropriate, I laugh out loud. His intentional jokes are funny, and he likes to hear us laugh. Before the brain tumour, he would love people to laugh at his jokes and that hasn't changed. So if I feel the need for a little respite from the heaviness of the day, the best way to find it is by interacting with my son.

Winnie interacted well with him. I frequently walked past his room when she was attending to him. The door would be closed because she respected his privacy, but I would hear them chitchatting away, she with her endearing manner, and he with his courteous quips. No wonder they called him Gentleman Craig. As his illness intensified, he wasn't quite so chirpy, but he didn't fail to greet her with a spring in his voice, until his voice faded into a whisper. Bathing had become an ordeal for him before Winnie came along, and it appeared that he was not partial to bed bathing either. Everything was an effort. Winnie recounted numerous occasions when he would try to smooth talk her out of bathing him.

"Craigie," she would say, "Your mother will kill me if she finds out I haven't bathed you properly."

"My mother doesn't have to know," he would retort, "I won't tell if you don't. Can't you just wipe my face clean?"

The banter would continue for a while, then Winnie would bluff him that she'd given in, by saying that she'd shave him and brush his teeth, and that would suffice. He'd be happy with that, and the two of them would make small talk during the course of the facial spruce up. As he was chatting away, she would shrewdly begin to wash the other parts of his body. By the time he realised what was going on, it was too late!

"Ah Winnie," he'd protest, "you promised you wouldn't bath me today!"

"Sorry Craig," she'd say, "but I'm scared of your mother."

Winnie laughed when she told me that story. It happened quite often, she said. I still smile when I think about it. He was like a little boy, and one never knew if it was a brain thing, or if he was playing the fool. It was best not to know really.

On days when I was home, I would hear Winnie laughing behind closed doors, and I would silently grin, wondering what the joke was this time. It didn't seem real that I could laugh one minute, and cry the next. I struggled with the notion that a GBM brain tumour could destroy a person's body. This type of cancer could not spread to other parts of the body, so why was he so thin and frail? It was logical—he wasn't eating, but I hadn't expected that. He was a shadow of the man he used to be. His shirt size had gone from XXL to medium, and he was still losing weight. There'd be nothing left of him. He was so ill that if we switched off his radio for any reason, he wouldn't ask for it to be turned on again. And he did so love his radio. He wasn't even asking for his glasses. He might request a cigarette, but would only take one puff, then tell us to stub it out, and keep it for next time. He always was a "waste not, want not" person. I was able to deal far better with Craig's mind than I was with his body, probably because I expected his mind to deteriorate, but his body was a different kettle of fish.

Sunday, 17 June 2012

This afternoon he asked me to check on the prices of photocopies. He used to make copies for customers who came into his shop. I was glad I'd worked there, because I understood the business. I could tell that we were about to embark on another of those conversations which would ultimately reveal that he had something on his mind, so I told him I'd check the prices in the book. He warned me to be careful because some people didn't pay.

"Who?" I asked, "Customers?"

"Yes," He replied, "and other people."

"Like who?"

No answer. I asked if the family paid and he said no. That gave me the impression that he had grievances with family members, so I named each one that I could think of. Does this one pay, does that one pay? He said no to all of them. I was afraid to ask about myself, but I did.

"Do I pay?"

He hesitated, and then said, "Not always." Oh my, did he have an axe to grind with all of us?

"Are you cross with these people?" I asked.

"Yes."

My analytical mind told me that he had some form of resentment towards his family, so I suggested that he forgive them, and he agreed. I took his hand and led him in a prayer of forgiveness. A sense of calm came over him, and I too was at peace.

I gave a lot of thought to that conversation afterwards. If his brain had been normal, the subject would probably never have arisen, in which case he may have died with bitterness in his heart, but now he was at peace with himself, and with his family. I'll never know why he was angry, but I don't need to. The point is, he was now content, and if my perception of his uneasiness was, perchance, an illusion, then it doesn't matter.

Monday, 18 June 2012

Winnie says her patient kept calling for me today. That's not unusual, he calls me often. Each time she went to him, he told her he wasn't calling her, but his mother, and each time she explained to him that I was at work, and she was attending him. But he didn't remember what she'd said. In the end, she had a brain wave and told him that it was Monday. He showed immediate cognition, remembering that I work on Mondays and he didn't ask for me again. I found that quite phenomenal. When I arrived home, I went in to say hello. He didn't realise I hadn't been there all day, so reacted as though I had. I left his room and soon afterwards he called me. Ian went in to him and Craig informed him he wanted Mom and not Dad! When I went in, all he asked was what I was doing. I think he was trying to assure himself of my presence. What I've related here is exactly what Sister Debbie had expected he would do if he were to be admitted to the hospice. Because I'm the person who's had the most personal contact with him over the past few months, and maybe because I'm his mother and he's become somewhat childlike, he would be expecting me to be around, and if I were not, he would get agitated and stressed. He knows I'll come home after a working day, but he doesn't expect me to be gone for longer than that, and even in his muddled state of mind, he would be continually asking for me until I appeared, and subsequently checking to make sure I was still around.

Each day I learn more about the human brain, and each day I am more intrigued. My non-medical opinion regarding cases of this type of brain damage, and I would think this includes Alzheimer's, because I detect similarities to what Craig has, is that if we take time to try and decipher what the patient is saying, rather than fob it off as insanity, we could save the patient, and ourselves, a lot of frustration. An example of this was the discussion I had with Craig recently when he called me to say that I must sort out the "plug". I tried, by questioning him, to establish what this "plug" was, or what its function was. Was it connected to the heater? No. Was it connected to the radio? No. There were no other appliances in the room, so I asked him what it was connected to.

"The cable," was his reply.

Ah, my mind told me, the only ostensible "cable" was the pipe that connected his urine bag to the condom. I put his hand on the pipe, and he confirmed that this was the "cable". Therefore the "plug" must be the condom. I left the room to find Ian and ask him to help me adjust the apparatus, but by the time I returned, Craig was holding the condom in his hand, rather tightly. This confirmed that it had probably not been slipping off in the night, but that he was constantly pulling it off.

"You don't like that thing, do you?" I asked.

"No."

"Okay, we won't be using it again."

At that point, Ian walked into the room.

"What now?" I asked.

Ian shrugged his shoulders and lent over to adjust the nappy, which was half undone. This turned out to be another one of those occasions when we had to change the bed linen and Craig's clothes in the middle of the night. We were both worn out, especially Ian, who gets up at 4:30 a.m. daily, in order to miss the peak hour traffic on his way to work each morning. Then Winnie came up with a grand suggestion.

"You can get special pads," she told us, "Not nappy liners; they are too thin. These are thicker pads that you put inside the nappy. Make sure you get the ones for men."

"Eureka!" I told myself, "Another solution! Hope this one works!"

I think there's a price war within the nappy industry, but I put on my boxing gloves, and after returning the expensive pads that I bought to their rightful owners, I managed to find a much cheaper source, and have since discovered another shop with discounted prices on medical gear, so, with a little help from my friends, I am not only the fastest trained nurse on the planet, but also the craftiest wheeler and dealer! The pads are working well, and thus far there's been a lot less usage of the washing machine. And all this because I worked out what a "plug" was.

I may sound ridiculously light hearted, but once again, it's my way of dealing with a highly stressful situation. Craig is a fragment of the man he used to be. I can't bear to go into the room when Winnie is bed bathing him. I touch his face and his hands because I can't bear not to. He's my son and I love him so much, but his fingers are spindly and his cheekbones protrude where once two rounded cheeks embraced laughing lips that used to tell hilarious stories about Lovemore, the unpretentious Zimbabwean national, who did crazy things. My heart is broken.

Tuesday, 19 June 2012

The headaches were bad today, which seems to be rather the exception than the rule lately. I gave him one of the schedule seven painkillers, but twenty minutes later he was still suffering.

"How bad is the headache?" I asked.

His brain tells him to use logical phrases, like, "It's more than one headache."

I have established that many headaches all at once, constitute a very bad headache, so I popped him another pill. I've been forced to overcome my phobia about pills, but it's still difficult for me to administer two of these killer tablets in less than half an hour. Another half hour went by, and he was still murmuring about his headache, so I popped him a paracetemol, which is usually ineffective, but it did the trick; or was it a psychological thing? For whatever reason, he slept peacefully after that.

So how do we get through the hours, the days and the weeks? This is Craig's journey, and yet it's our journey too—Ian's and mine. We're walking it alongside our son, and it pains us both, knowing that the boy we raised will soon be leaving. We have walked in faith, hope and love—God's love, which continues to carry us through. On days when I have felt drained of all that is within me, He has lifted me up, and given me hope of a better life for Craig in the loving arms of Jesus. God has given me His Word that the night is nearly over, the day is almost here, and with that in mind, I can raise my hands to Heaven every morning, and thank Him for a brand new day.

Chapter 24

Debbie, our daughter, regularly phones from England, to find out how her brother is. She recently phoned my mobile to speak to him. He chatted a bit and she had rather a lot to say. Later Ian asked him if Debbie had phoned. We like to establish what he remembers. Occasionally he will recall a recent incident. In reply to Ian's question, he said, "Debbie? No, she was here."

I didn't know whether to be happy or sad, but happy was a better idea. It was good that he thought Debbie had been to visit him.

Saturday, 23 June 2012

It's early evening and I go into his room to see how he's doing. He's wide awake. The eyes are open, and I can tell by the look on his face that he's anxious.

"Are you okay Craig?"

No reply. What a stupid question, I tell myself.

"Would you like me to sit with you for a while?"

"If you like." That means yes, but I don't want to bother you.

I sit beside him on the bed, taking his hand in mine. He has long fingers, and I stroke them. I will never forget his hands. There doesn't seem to be anything to say. I ask myself what on earth a mother can say to her dying son, and my thoughts are screaming again. I've told him how much we love him, how much Jesus loves him. I've said everything I can think of to comfort him. I've read to him; I've sung to him; I've held him in my arms, as I did when he was little. In many ways he is a child again. It's easy to talk to a child, and I've been allowed to recollect those childhood moments, and to kiss his cheek without being told he's too old for that. His hand tightens around mine, and I lean back on the bed, propping myself up on an elbow, as I ease closer to him.

"We're very proud of you," I say for the millionth time, "The whole family. We're all so proud of you."

"Why?" He never gives himself credit for anything.

"For the way you've handled your illness," I say.

Again, he doesn't answer.

I look at his fragile arms. I can easily close my thumb and middle finger around his wrists. I can't do that to myself, and my wrists are relatively small. His hand tightens around mine again, and he's reluctant to let go. I am sobbing uncontrollably, those same voiceless tears that I've mastered so well.

On the inside of his bedroom door is a copy of a nineteenth century painting by Holman Hunt. It's called "The Light of the World." I bought it some years ago at St. Paul's Cathedral in London, where one of the two originals hangs. On the back of the picture are some reflections on its background and message, which is based on a verse from the New Testament, Revelation 3:20—"Here I am! I stand at the door and knock. If anyone hears my voice and opens the door, I will come in and eat with him and he with me." Holman Hunt has portrayed Jesus

Christ, the Light of the World, standing outside the door of the individual's heart of life, and over the years this has resulted in many people receiving Christ the Saviour into their lives. The review illustrates the meaning of the painting's details, which are based on Scripture, and are certainly a revelation of the love of God, so much so, that the painter himself forsook his agnosticism whilst painting.

I'm looking at the picture and thanking God for my son's life. His Son has knocked at the door of my son's heart, and my son has allowed Him in. I think he's asleep now, so I stand up to leave. He stirs and squeezes my hand lightly.

"I'll always be here for you Craig," I say, "I may go out from time to time, but I will come back, I promise you."

"Thanks," he says quietly, and I know he means it.

I lovingly recall the many tête-à-têtes we used to have whilst sitting in waiting rooms at the hospital. How far away and long ago that seems. Was it another world, another life? I see his frailty, and I try to remind myself of that big fellow, whose hands would work on motor vehicle engines. I see him on the roof, rigging the satellite dish for our TV, and rushing to the rescue in a thunderstorm when Ian was away and our house alarm sound-blasted the neighbourhood, after being struck by lightning.

I release my hand from his. He stirs again.

"I will come back, my boy, I promise."

There's a toilet roll on the table and I grab a long piece, because I need it.

"Thanks, Mom," he says, and I wonder if he heard me tearing the toilet tissue. He used to tell me not to cry when the time comes, because dying is a part of life and we all have to do it. I don't know how I'm going to remember that.

I walk into the lounge. There's unopened mail lying on the kist. I smile when I look at the familiar handwriting. It's another card from Denise. She's the sister of a friend, and she was cured of cancer a few years ago. She regularly sends cards of encouragement, with little verses from the Bible. Like so many others, she has blessed our lives. I wish I could mention everyone, but all will remain dear to me. These people are my rainbows.

Ian's in the kitchen, cooking supper—again. He does a lot of that nowadays. There are loads of blessings in my life, loads. The hardships are unfathomable, but so too are the blessings. What did I do to deserve them? Nothing. I tell myself to focus more on the positive things.

Sunday, 24 June 2012

Doug came to visit this morning, but there was no response from Craig whatsoever. It broke Doug's heart to look at him. He clung to me like the big bear that he is and neither of us had anything to say, but we were both crying. Tomorrow will be my big bear's fifty first birthday. I'm holding a birthday gift for my eldest son in one hand and a wave goodbye to my second son in the other. It's not surprising that something feels horribly wrong.

This afternoon Brian and Nicky came. Craig managed, with some effort, to greet them. He struggled to talk, but no one could make out what he was saying. I told both his brothers to hold his hand, because I think his sense of touch is a little better than any of his other senses. I detect that he's losing hearing in the left ear, as he doesn't always respond to sound, which although probably due to his brain not picking up the signals, could also be pressure on his ears. I think he feels a sense of security when we hold his hand; he seems to take comfort from it.

I can't stop thinking about how sympathetic he used to be towards the many brain damaged individuals we encountered in the neurosurgical clinic, secretly sensing that someday he too may be like that. I knew this would be painful, but I had no idea how painful. It eats into your heart; it pounds your head; it gnaws your stomach; it tears your body apart, and it turns slumber into a succession of frenzied dreams, which, on awakening, prove not to be dreams after all. This is a reality, and it won't depart from us. Ian and I are trying to behave normally. We're trying to hold normal conversations, to cook normal meals, to watch normal television, to take a normal bath, and to play with our normal dog. It's not working. This state of affairs is not normal. It's all-consuming, with no way out. We simply try to focus on helping our son to the best of our ability. Winnie is doing her best too. She says brushing Craig's teeth is challenging, because he won't, or can't, spit out. There are so many different aspects to consider.

Sunday, 1st July 2012

What a ghastly day! Ian hasn't been flying on Sundays recently; we don't do much of anything outside of our home. I went to church in the morning, and when I came home, Brian and Nicky arrived. Brian was talking to Craig, and then came out to tell me that Craig had said he wanted to go to the toilet. I knew that meant it was already too late, so I asked Nicky to make the tea while Ian and I attended to Craig. Oh my word! It was the biggest disaster we have yet contended with. I don't want to degrade Craig's dignity, but this is the actuality of an incapacitating disease. Nurses handle it constantly, but Craig is our adult son, and I cannot describe the emotional horror of such an undertaking. Fortunately, Craig was unaware of what was taking place. He didn't know what happened and he didn't know what was being done about it. For him to be embarrassed about it, would, I think, destroy me.

Doug arrived in the middle of the calamity, and I told him to join Brian and Nicky for tea. When the crisis was over, they were able to visit with him, but he wasn't responsive at all. Later that afternoon, Ian and I went through the same motions all over again. Questions were once again raised about whether we should admit Craig to Hospice, but I think I would find that even more unnerving than dealing with the disasters at home. He is only partially lucid, but he would know, and I sense he'd be highly disorientated. I don't want that. He's dealing with more than his share as it is. The mental and physical strain of this ordeal is enormous for both Ian and me, but I think it would be worse if we let him go to Hospice. They are caring people, they are gracious, loving people, but I doubt that would be a favourable environment for Craig's particular type of illness. Hospice ordinarily only admit patients to their care a fortnight before they consider that they are going to pass away. According to the various stages of dying, they are fairly good at ascertaining the status of their patients. Craig is a very unusual patient. Sister Debbie thought he would pass away some time before his condition worsened as much as it has. She says he has incredible stamina and will to live. Each time I've been to the hospital to collect his medication the neurosurgeons have expressed their amazement that he's still alive. He's so thin and weak that it's inconceivable that his organs are still functional.

Monday, 2 July 2012

Could anything be worse than yesterday? The answer is yes. This morning I received news from Australia that my mother had passed away. She hadn't been well for a few weeks, so I was anticipating bad news, but it still came as a shock. In two weeks' time, on Nelson Mandela's birthday, she would have been ninety-one. How pleased my brother Tony and I are that we celebrated her ninetieth birthday with her last year. Our sister, Jane, was with her when she died peacefully, but how sad we are for Jane, who is contending with everything on her own. Life dishes out some hard knocks. I was at work when I received the call from Jane, so I packed up and left the office, but I couldn't face going home, where I knew I'd have to face my dying son. My mother was dead; my son was dying. In my mind, the world had turned on itself. And when would I have time to grieve for my mother? When?

From the office, I drove to Edith's flat, where we chatted over tea for a couple of hours, before I made my weary way home, exhausted from sheer mental anguish. Ian had some nice things to say about my mother, which made me smile, because she was a crazy person, whose melodramatic life lent itself to the most unpredictable occurrences in all creation. My mother was matchless. My father called her a daredevil of note. In her younger days, one wouldn't contemplate daring her to do anything, because the more drastic the dare was, the more likely she was to do it. She strived to be the centre of attraction, and she was. Yet, aside from her unconventionality, she had an ability second to none to write and speak the Queen's English in a manner befitting to royalty itself, or so she would have us believe. Her father was an Irish Australian, descended from Charles II of England—illegitimately, of course; but that made us into a noble family, which was probably why my father married her. He, you see, was an unqualified snob, an officer and a gentleman, who was awarded the Military Cross for bravery in the Second World War, which was probably why my mother married him. I don't think there was any love lost, or gained, between them, and yet I loved them both. They had two kids, and after the divorce, she remarried and had two more kids. Lots and lots of things happened, but in the end, she outlived both husbands. Perchance these short memoirs are my brief opportunity to mourn my fun-loving mother, who despite her outward appearance, also went through the school of hard knocks, and sadly, never managed to defeat her demons. I hope she's at peace now. I would like to think she's waiting to embrace her grandson in a place where there are no tears, and the streets are paved with gold.

Tuesday, 3 July 2012

Tony's coming for dinner tonight. We want to celebrate our mother together. Nicky will be coming too, because Brian's in

Cape Town on business. Tony is a musician and I've asked him to sing at Craig's funeral, which seems bizarre, in a way. How can I be arranging his funeral ahead of time? But I am. I want him to go soon; he's suffering so much. I know that I'll miss him, and I can't bear the thought of him not being with us, yet I want him to go. This will never make sense. I want him to stay as much as I want him to go. How do I get my head around this perplexity? I want him here, but not like this, and I therefore acknowledge that it's time for him to leave.

I chose the hymns for the memorial service some time ago. I want our son's final farewell to be beautiful, as was the day of his arrival on this earth. I want everything to be right.

Wednesday, 4th July 2012

I think this week was destined to be one of the worst of my life. Our dinner arrangements last night didn't turn out the way we'd planned. Shortly before 5:00 p.m., Ian and I decided to turn Craig in his bed and attend to his personal requirements before settling down with our guests. For the past few days he'd developed a cough, the only apparent reason for which would seem that his whole body is shutting down. As Ian lifted him to change his nappy, he began a violent coughing fit. The nappy changing was abandoned, as we struggled to settle him. The coughing got progressively worse, and he began to choke, with violent vocal reverberations which didn't stop. Tony rushed to our assistance, but the incident grew more horrific. I grabbed my cell phone and tried to contact Sister Debbie, to no avail, so I phoned Lindy. She and Doug were at our house in fifteen minutes. By then Craig had calmed down a little, but his breathing was still exaggerated by the heavy coughing and vocal noises. Nicky arrived to find everyone around his bed. We all assumed he was dying. Lindy said his pulse was strong, so his heart was fine, but everything else appeared to indicate the end. We were basically saying our goodbyes, which was the most awful thing I've ever done in my life. I was traumatised. Craig was unable to speak and was seemingly oblivious to what was going on around him. His face was deathly white. I cannot describe what went on in his room that evening.

After about an hour and a half, his breathing subsided. One by one the family left the room, leaving one person at a time to watch him. I'd cooked a large pot of lamb stew, so everyone stayed for supper. Sister Debbie contacted us and spoke to Lindy. It was agreed that Craig had had a seizure. He was unable to cough up the phlegm that was sitting in his chest, so that had made the problem substantially worse.

By 9:00 p.m. everyone had gone home. Ian set the alarm clock to wake us every two hours throughout the night, so that we could turn Craig onto his other side, thus preventing the phlegm from staying in one place, thereby causing another coughing fit. I was petrified that he would choke to death. His night was fairly comfortable, but Ian and I didn't sleep at all.

This morning Sister Debbie paid her weekly visit. She suggested that Craig has probably moved into the next phase of dying. I don't think those were her exact words, but essentially that was what she meant. She has a gentle way of speaking to families, and I've grown very fond of her over the few months that she's been attending to our son. She was telling me that she'd lost nine patients in the past fortnight. Hospice workers are extraordinary people. Debbie chats to Craig with a deep sense of empathy, and he has developed a sincere appreciation of her. I'm sure she's like that with all her patients, which makes me wonder how she copes with their imminent deaths. She has watched Craig change from a well-built man to no more than a skin coated skeleton. I realise that is a hideous description, but it's the brazen truth, which smashes my heart to pieces. I try continually to avert the tendency to lean on my own understanding of my son's predicament, as I watch every bone protruding from his limp body, and I listen to Ian's constant lament that this is so cruel.

My dear friend Dawn often comes to visit.

Recently she asked, "You don't ask God why, do you, Léonie?"

"Not why he got a tumour," I answered, "But I am starting to ask why it's taking so long."

That's a question to which I'll probably never get an answer. I have to remind myself that the reason for no answer is probably because I wouldn't be capable of comprehending it. I can only ask God to grant Ian and me the strength to get through each day, and ultimately to wipe out the picture of suffering that we face daily, that we might retain the memory of our robust son, who was once as normal as normal is.

Friday 6th July 2012

A strange phenomenon occurred yesterday. Since his seizure, Craig has been quieter than usual. For the past week he hasn't been calling for me, in fact, he hasn't been calling at all. We frequently ask him if he has any needs, and his reaction is commonly a slight shake of the head. Yesterday he graced me with conversation.

"Is your door open?" he asked. He speaks very quietly now, because speaking is such an effort.

"Which door?" I asked.

No answer, so I indulged him by saying I'd shut the door.

"Can't you smell fish?" he asked.

Ian and I had had fish for supper, but I hadn't offered him any, because he always says no. It wasn't a strong smelling fish, but he must have smelt it. I asked him if he wanted some, hoping he'd say no, because it was finished. He replied that he didn't, but because he was asking about food, I asked if he was hungry. He didn't reply, so I asked him if he'd like some soup. It's a case of re-wording the question. By doing that, I'm hopeful that his brain can pick up what I'm trying to get through to him. The word 'soup' obviously triggered some recognition.

"What kind have you got?"

"Tomato."

To my astonishment, he said he'd try some. I rushed to the kitchen and made up a cup of instant tomato soup, which I fed to him. He ate the whole lot.

"Would you like a slice of bread?" I ventured to ask.

"Just one slice, please," he replied.

Another mad rush to the kitchen ensued. I buttered the bread and cut the crusts off, because he doesn't have the energy to chew. Again he ate the lot. I reckon he'd have eaten more, but I was too afraid to ask him, for fear he might get sick. He hasn't eaten anything other than yoghurt for over two months, but I did offer him some milk with which to swallow his medication.

"Whatever you recommend," was his reply, which made me laugh, because he so seldom uses "complicated" words nowadays. His brain doesn't usually retain them. My laughter suddenly turned to remorse. Oh Lord, why should I get so excited when my almost forty-one-year-old son uses a big word like "recommend?" This is lunacy; the whole world has gone stark staring mad! I'm not living in this rotten dream, I'm not. I'm not! But it's real; I have to accept that it's real.

I smiled a little. "I recommend some warm milk, my boy. Then you can go to sleep. Or perhaps you'd like to me to read to you for a while?"

"Yes please."

Lucid moments are so precious. After Ian and I had administered the milk and the medication and the nappy change and the turning over to the other side, I took his Bible and read from the book of Revelation, that beautiful passage about the New Jerusalem, and again I told him about the place we both believe he's going to. I prayed for him to have a peaceful night, then kissed his cheek and stood up to leave.

"Love you Craig," I said.

"Love you too."

Today he had another cup of soup and another slice of bread. It's very hard to know what's happening in his body. Nothing makes any sense.

Chapter 25

From time to time Winnie takes a few days off to visit her family in her home town. She always sends a stand-in caregiver. Faith came once in June, but she's no longer available, so Merriam comes. She's a very sweet lady, with a magnificent singing voice. Whenever she arrives in the mornings, she walks into Craig's room and sings beautiful gospel songs to him. What a blessing that is! Like Winnie, she chats to Craig and he thoroughly enjoys her little talks. She often comes and tells me what he's been saying to her, and I find it rather amusing. One time she asked me who Belinda was, because Craig had been muttering that name. I could only recall one Belinda that Craig knew, but I asked him who she was.

Without hesitation, he said, "My brother's wife."

I asked who his brother was, to which he replied that it was Doug.

Well, he does have a brother called Doug, but his wife is Lindy. I thought he might be confused, so I asked if he meant Lindy.

No," he asserted, "Belinda."

"Who is your brother?"

"Doug," he affirmed.

Brian has a childhood friend called Douglas, whose wife is called Belinda. As adults, Douglas became a good friend of Craig as well. When he was growing up, I adored Douglas, and would repeatedly tell him that he was my fourth son. As he grew older, that became a constant, and the whole family knew how fond I was of young Doug, and that he was considered another of my sons.

I quizzed Craig. "How many brothers do you have?"

He stunned me by asking, "Called Doug?"

"Yes," I said.

"Two." How wonderful that was! Despite his utter confusion, he was very clear about his "adopted" brother.

It's very difficult to ascertain exactly how much damage there is to Craig's brain. I do my utmost to recognise his needs, but there are occasions when I become a little flummoxed by what he says or how he reacts to my questions. One day, when his mind seemed more muddled than usual, I asked him if he knew who I was.

His answer was simply, "Isn't that rather a stupid question?"

I smiled, because I didn't want to hear any other answer.

Reminders of Craig's former life are everywhere. There was a day in July when the printer on my desk at the office wasn't working properly. Someone suggested we have it serviced, so I asked our handyman, Joe, to drop it off at a place in Benoni, where Craig used to buy supplies for his shop. Because it's quite near to where we live, I regularly used to go there to collect his urgent orders, and he would pick them up from our house on his way home from work. The business is owned by a lovely couple, with whom I had become quite friendly over the past two or three years. When Craig was in hospital, or having treatment, they would ask after him, and I know they were fond of him because they were concerned about his wellbeing. This morning Michelle phoned to say the printer was ready, so I said I'd pick it up later.

I parked the car outside their gate, and as I lifted the latch to walk into the yard, I felt my heart leap. Silly, I thought, I don't have an issue with coming here, so why am I feeling like this? I walked through their workshop, which was filled with printers and cartridges, and into the office. Clint and Michelle were both there to greet me. Suddenly the whole world came crashing down on my head. I was bombarded with recollections of Craig filling cartridges and testing printers. I could hear him talking to the loyal customers who would come into his shop simply for a chat, as they were passing by. In split seconds I was recalling days when I worked in the shop whilst he was having radiation treatment. His regular customers would come in and ask after him. They told me how much they liked him, and how he would bend over backwards to assist them. They said I should be very proud of him, the way he would speak positively about his condition, even when his head was full of clips, and they knew he was in pain. One lady told me she wished he was her son. I was terribly glad he wasn't.

I hadn't seen Clint and Michelle for months. I tried to move towards one of them to give them a hug, but my feet seemed to be stuck to the floor. Tears were gushing out of my eyes, and my voice had become defunct. Clint came forward to hug me, and I managed a blubbing, "I'm so sorry. This is so embarrassing."

"It's okay," Michelle said, "It's okay," and she too was tearful. I cannot even type this without crying, and this has not happened throughout the writing of this book. Right now I'm not the in the least bit concerned about writing the good old Queen's

English, or where to put the punctuation marks. I'm writing what I'm feeling, which is rotten. Rotten, rotten, rotten.

"Sit down," Clint was saying, "I'm going to make you a cup of tea." I love Clint and Michelle. I calmed down, and ended up staying for half an hour, updating them on what had been happening. Craig never used to charge me for refilling my cartridges. He taught me to do the simple ones myself and would supply free ink. He did the colour ones for me, because they are harder to fill. If I required a new cartridge, he'd give it to me at cost, or more often, for no charge. I bought a new cartridge for my home printer from Clint that day. He gave it to me at the wholesale price that he would have charged Craig's business. He said he'd never charge me full price. That was a precious moment for me.

I told a few people about my day. I cried every time I told the story, and Ian said I should stop talking about it, but I couldn't. I think that's the difference between men and women. Women let it all out, men suffer in silence. In the same way, I won't be able to stop talking about my middle son after he's gone, but one day the crying will become less. People who've been through this tell me it will. They say there'll come a time when my thoughts about my son will be smiley ones.

Some folk don't know what to say to Ian and me anymore, and I find myself trying to console them, but that's okay, because I understand how they feel. They don't want to visit Craig because they can't bear to look at him. That's understandable too. We weren't designed to look upon emaciated bodies without recoiling. It's not something anyone would want to keep in mind. That's why some months ago I framed the happiest photograph of my boy that I have, and placed it above the television set, so that I would look at it often. I make a point of focusing on it time and time again whilst I'm watching TV. That is the face I want to keep in my mind all the days of my life. After he's gone, I will continue to look at that photo every day. That is the Craig I know. That is the Craig I will remember.

Ian looks at that happy face too. It was taken on Christmas Day a couple of years ago. He was wearing a paper hat out of a Christmas cracker. Ian doesn't talk much, but the time would come when he would stand up and tell of his son's brave journey with a debilitating disease, and how proud we both were to have been called his parents.

On that day, Doug and Brian would recount their sentiments in moving tributes to their brother. Nicky would share Brian's sentiments by saying how proud he was to be the little brother of a humble, grateful and kind person, whom God had used to do amazing things. Brian would relate stories of their childhood escapades, and speak with love about his awesome brother, Craig. Doug was to talk about the most selfless person he had ever known, a man who was genuinely concerned about things most people say they care about, but in actuality do not. He would say that Craig cared about the wellbeing of those around him; no matter that he may have suffered through their selfishness, and he would speak of an honest, committed-to-serve person, who respected all around him, adding that he was one of the best friends Lindy ever had. Everyone would call attention to the fact that Craig never said, "Why me?"

Monday, 9 July 2012

Craig's been particularly quiet for the past few days. When his brothers visit him, he says practically nothing. This must be very hard for them, but one thing is certain; they have many happy memories of the way their brother was.

Brian's going to Cape Town again tomorrow. He has to go every week this month, and then he's going to America for the whole of August. This will be a major career move for him, and he will not be able to come home if his brother passes away. Poor Brian has agonised over the likelihood of this happening, but we have to accept that it could. I so want both my other sons here when that moment comes. I don't even want to think about one of them not being here, but sadly it's another one of those blatant possibilities.

I was busy writing the above, when Brian and Nicky arrived with their new Miniature Schnauzer puppy. What a little bundle of fluff! He has furrier eyebrows than the Edwards boys, and theirs are quite admirable! His name is Zoro. I ask myself why I do things that I know will make people cry, but I was compelled to show Zoro to Craig. I placed the little dog near his cheek, and it sniffed around his face. Craig immediately withdrew his right hand from beneath the blankets, moving it towards the little dog. What a heart-wrenching moment. I placed Zoro by his hand, and he began to gently scratch the little fellow. Oh my God, will I ever stop weeping? Brian too was fighting back the tears. He and Nicky said goodbye and love you to Craig, who managed a quiet, "Love you too." Nicky took the puppy and we walked into the lounge, at which point I threw my arms around my youngest child, and sobbed. His embrace was comforting indeed. What bitter sweet pain!

After they left, I clutched on to Ian, with a desperate, "I can't do this anymore," coming from my vocal cords.

"Do you want him to go to Hospice?" Ian said, because there was nothing else to say.

"No. That would be worse." And all the while I was wondering if anything could be worse than this. They call it Catch 22; I call it persecution.

I wiped a couple of tears away from Craig's face again this evening. He's far too weak to cry properly, but I swear his heart is crying on occasions when he's clear-headed. What goes through his mind to make him cry? Is he mindful of happy days when he was having fun? Did the puppy make him cry tonight? Was he thinking about his little dog, Bam, who had to be given away? Was he asking for his life back? *Oh my Lord, please take him home soon! There's a much better life waiting for him there.*

I opened my late father's old King James Bible tonight. I haven't looked at it for a long time. On the blank page in front is a hand-written verse from the friend who gave him the Bible in 1959.

> *The sun shall no more be thy light by day; neither for brightness shall the moon give light unto thee: but the Lord shall be unto thee an everlasting light, and thy God thy glory. (Isaiah 60:19).*

I was beginning to think God had stopped speaking to me. I paged through the Bible to the next verse, which says:

> *The sun shall no more go down, neither shall the moon withdraw itself: for the Lord shall be thine everlasting light, and the days of thy mourning shall be ended.*

Oh, how I want my days of mourning to be ended! It was also in the book of Isaiah where, almost four years ago, I found the Scripture about the Lord leading the blind in ways they had not known. Craig's vision was poor then, but he wasn't blind. Now he is, and that promise still stands. God said He would make darkness light and crooked things straight. I now think this will happen for Craig in a spiritual way.

Wednesday, 11th July 2012

We're still inundated with loving emails from friends around the world. That has never stopped, which is so encouraging. Lindy told me today that her whole family prayed for Craig last night. I've never felt alone during this ordeal. Even as I write, I know there are thousands of people who are undergoing similar experiences, and although some are worse than others, each person's burden is as great to him or her as anyone else's. I don't believe that anguish can be measured. Whose pain is worse—yours or mine? No one knows why we have to endure it, but I believe that one day, when this life is over, God will reveal that to us, and we will finally come to an understanding of how it worked for our good. It's human to cry, or shout, or throw things at walls occasionally; it's human to get angry and temperamental. I'm sure we all do those things. I do, but I'm convinced that if we take time to sit down and count our blessings, we will find that they outweigh those adversities that come to steal our joy. Many times I've had to remind myself of these principles.

Tracy came today. She's a nursing sister friend of Lindy's. She'd like to work for Hospice. She's been coming to visit Craig every week for the past two months. Once when she visited, she asked him if he was in pain. His reply was totally unexpected.

"No, but everyone else around here is a pain!"

Tracy was loath to tell me this, but she finally succumbed. As with so many of Craig's remarks, I found it amusing. Poor Craigie, we must drive him round the bend, fussing over him all the time, but what else should we do? Tracy was shocked to see how thin his face has become since she was here last Wednesday. She'd be a good hospice sister, full of compassion and a great nurse. For the past three days he's been very quiet, but still managed his, "Love you too," when she left. The first time she came, she brought him a lovely soft blanket, and I could swear he still remembers that she gave it to him. Some things will remain in his heart until he leaves us; like his love for Jesus. This I know.

Debbie phoned from England this evening. She told me that my fourteen-year-old grand-daughter, Kimberley, has written a beautiful song to Uncle Craig about his salvation. She plays the piano and sings, and she recorded it on her mobile phone. Her sister, Adelaide, also has an incredible amount of love and compassion for her uncle. Whenever I speak to her, she asks after him with a heart that appears too mature for a twelve year old. These are the positives in my life—my wonderful family and friends. I think of Barry and Linda, dear friends of forty something years. Linda keeps showing up with meals which come at exactly the right moment, when the last thing Ian and I feel like doing is cooking. We don't even feel like eating, until Linda's food appears. That couple have a special gift of helping those in need.

After Lisa, passed away, Edith often said she had days, and weeks, when she was "floating". That's what I'm doing right now, floating. You float, and you float, and you don't reach anywhere. You don't touch anything and nothing touches you. You have no destination and you don't know where you will land. But you keep going, and all being well, there will come a time when you are able to swim ashore.

Friday, 13 July 2012

I visited Edith this morning. I'm so grateful to my other kids for providing the means for us to have a caregiver. The family say I should get out a bit, even though I seldom have the desire to do so. I want to be close by for my boy, but I know I've to be a bit elastic, to stretch myself far away enough to get a break, but close enough to be able to spring back at any given moment. Edith is my crutch. I feel I'm being unfair to her by pouring out my woes, because it must force her to recall those awful memories of losing her own child, but she says I was there for her when Lisa was dying, and she wants to share my sorrow now. The thing is, we understand each other; we both know where the other one has been; we both appreciate the anguish. As mothers, we started out walking this road together, before we even knew our children were going to die. We were filled with hope and the belief that they'd be healed. In time, we came to realise that their healing was to be of the spirit, and not the body.

Our son is still eating. Today he had cup of soup, a slice of bread and a small piece of chicken, followed by a small bowl of fruit salad, which contained pawpaw, a tropical fruit, also called papaya. I mention it because each time I put a piece of this fruit in his mouth, he said, "Mmm, I need that!" expressing his special liking of that particular fruit. This prompted me to buy a whole pawpaw the following day. When he had finished the fruit salad, he ate a small piece of cake. If I previously had any understanding of his condition, it was expelled tonight. How does he not eat for nearly three months, and then suddenly start eating again? What this proves to me is that nothing is predictable. On one occasion when I offered him food, he wanted to know how much it cost. When I said it was free, he didn't believe me, so I told him someone had given it to me.

"In that case," he responded, "I'll have some." His mind was living in a place where he assumed his life was perfectly normal.

I was praying for him last night, the same prayer I say every night, that he would have a comfortable night, with no pain. I thought he was asleep, but after the prayer he uttered the words, "Thank you, Father. Amen." There is a myriad of awareness left in his brain.

Thursday, 19 July 2012

I fed him some butterscotch pudding this evening. The trouble was, there wasn't any more. After he'd eaten, I asked if I could read to him.

"Yes," he answered," and then can I have my pudding?"

Oh dear! I could not convince him that the pudding was finished. He gave me a long story that Edith had said there was no more pudding, and I said there was, and he knew there was more! The bottom line was that he didn't believe me. I promised on my life that I would make sure there was more tomorrow, but he carried on about it until I felt like bursting into tears. At last I did the horrid thing—I changed the subject, making him forget about the pudding. I will definitely make sure there is some for tomorrow. What a fiasco.

Friday, 20July 2012

Today we had some huge trees cut down in our garden. We were going to leave them till later in the year, but the house has been extremely cold this winter, because no sun could infiltrate. Added to that, the lawn had given up the ghost and died, also due to lack of sun. There was a massive tree outside Craig's room, and when I saw it fall, I actually shed some tears! Within minutes, the sun came flooding into Craig's room, and I wished we'd done it months ago. We'd had a heater going day and night in there, but that was no longer necessary. A little change can do wonders. That set me thinking about my own life. A lot of things are going to change, and I don't know how I'm going to adjust to that.

Chapter 26

My son's illness is tormenting me. It's churning my insides. I've tried to tell myself that it isn't about me; it's about him, about what *he's* feeling, lying in that bed, day after week, after month, not even knowing what day, or week, or month it is, and not caring. Some days I walk around the house in a stupor, pretending to myself that I'm looking for something to do. I have plenty to do; I just don't want to do it.

I visited my new pastor, André and his wife, Pat, at their home recently. God placed me in their church at exactly the right time. I'd been wishing I'd joined them sooner, but I'm fully aware that God's timing is right. I joined them towards the end of Craig's life, and they've supported me at a time in my own life when I'm grateful for all the spiritual backing I can get. However, I believe that God's purpose in our relationship extends far beyond my present crisis. I don't know why I feel this way, but I do.

Friday, 27 July 2012—Email

Craig's brain has taken yet another inexplicable turn. For the past four days he has said no more than two words a day and that with great difficulty. On Monday he had a strange tremor which could have been a mild stroke, but his twisted face went back to normal afterwards. He could hardly talk for the next few days. Tracy visited and when she left, as usual, she told him she loved him. For the first time he did not respond to her, so she put her cheek to his and asked, "Do you love me, Craigie?"

"Always," he replied, much to the delight of all of us.

He went back to eating practically nothing, and slept most of the time. When he was awake, he appeared to be in pain, but was not able to say so. Once when I asked him if he had a headache, he struggled to get his hand out of the blankets and lift it to his forehead, denoting that he was in pain, so I gave him a painkiller. The headaches went on for the next couple of days. Prior to that, he had not had a headache for weeks. Yesterday Ian was with him all day, and he didn't say a single word. Once again, it seemed he was nearing the end, but I've learned not to assume that. At about 7:00 p.m. last night, I fed him some soup and bread, which he ate in silence. Then I asked if he had a headache. About a minute later, he suddenly opened his mouth and said,

"I don't have a headache."

I told him I was glad to hear him talking, and he stared at me in an odd fashion, asking why. The dialogue continued for a while. After Ian and I had eaten our dinner, I went back to his room. He was still wide awake. As usual, he had difficulty understanding me. At 10:00 p.m. we turned him over, and made him comfortable for the night. I felt really proud that he didn't have a single bed sore, after all these months of being bedridden. Ian left the room and I asked Craig if he was okay.

"Yes," he said, "But please can I have some cigarette?" His speech and thoughts are so jumbled now that he seems to know what he wants, but cannot put it into the right words. He hasn't smoked for about a month, so I gently told him that I was going to bed, and would let him smoke tomorrow. I nearly fell over backwards at his next word,

"Eish!!" (This is a typically African word, which roughly translates to "oh my goodness!") I was a little baffled, so I sat down and talked to him. The dialogue wasn't entirely sensible, but some of it was. This morning he was still able to talk. I was telling Merriam that we had bought some new nappies. Craig asked who they were for. When I told him they were for him, he looked horrified, which told us that he had no recollection of using nappies, and now it was a problem for him. I felt dreadful. I certainly didn't mean to embarrass him. Fortunately he soon got over it, because of his short term memory, and when Merriam was bathing him I could hear the two of them having a good old heart to heart. She told me afterwards that he had said she should go to the races, and if she took some friends, she'd be safe!

This is very difficult to fathom. Personally, I think that tumour shifts, I've been saying that for a long time. For the past few days it's been pressurising his speech area, and now it has moved and he's talking more sense than he has for weeks. I cannot verify my theory; it's just an amateur observation, an uneducated guess. I've been trying to analyse this for months, and I do think I am able to make some sense out of it.

Saturday, 28 July 2012

He was scrambling his words today, talking to himself about someone called Sharon. When I quizzed him about her, I managed to ascertain, after much probing, that she worked in the shopping centre where his shop was. He said she was a hairdresser, and that they were talking about dresses. That could have been an association of ideas. I asked if she bought cartridges from him, and he said not yet. I asked if the centre was busy and he said not really.

"Would you like me to work in the shop?" I asked. "Maybe you want to go somewhere?"

"Yes please," he said.

"Where do you need to go?" I indulged him.

He thought for a moment, and then said he didn't know.

"Just take a day off," I smiled, "and I'll work."

"Okay, thanks."

I told him I'd have to know the prices for customers' faxing.

"They're all in the book," he said confidently, and I knew he was delighted to be getting a day off work. He used to work hard, seven days a week, and a day off was a rarity.

Then he asked for orange juice, and when I offered him more, he said, "May as well 'cause, I'm not paying for it."

He's got a thing about how much the food costs, which I believe goes back to the days when he was running his own household.

It was as though he was living in another time, playing it all out in his mind. How I wished I could indeed get in my car and go work in his shop, like I used to. That would mean everything would be the same as it used to be. But is that what I wanted? No, because that would mean I'd still have to face today. What a bunch of crazy mixed up notions! One starts to think like that when things like this happen. Oh Craigie! Can't we just have a big fight, or something? Can't you just argue with me, like you used to? That would prove that things were normal and nothing had changed. But it has and there's nothing anyone will ever be able to do about it.

Written the following week

On Sunday night, I received a text message from my daughter Debbie, quoting Psalm 91: 14-16. (NIV)

> *"Because he loves me", says the Lord, "I will rescue him; I will protect him, for he acknowledges my name. He will call upon me and I will answer him; I will be with him in trouble, I will deliver him and honour him. With long life I will satisfy him and show him my salvation."*

I believe that was a promise from God for Craig and I knew that, for him, long life meant an eternity in Heaven. I hoped that he was calling upon the Lord, because I believed God was ready to take him home.

On Monday, 30 July I went to work as usual. Craig was very quiet in the morning when I said goodbye to him. Knowing that I worked with Doug, Winnie made the decision to phone him and not me.

He came into my office, and all he said was, "Come, we must go."

A feeling of dizziness came over me, and someone brought me a glass of water. Doug wouldn't let me drive my car, so I went with him. Winnie had said that Craig had taken a turn for the worse, but we didn't know what that meant. Doug called the whole family, and one by one they arrived at our home. Craig wasn't responding to anything. It appeared he'd had a slight seizure, and his breathing had become very erratic, but it was soon clear that this was not the same as the previous seizure. Sister Debbie arrived and informed us that she thought he was nearing the end. He was agitated and apparently in some degree of pain, so she went off to get a morphine pump. A small needle was inserted below his shoulder, and a low dose of morphine was pumped in through a tube, at regular intervals. Sister Debbie showed Ian how to administer the morphine, explaining that it would stop any pain, but its main purpose was to de-traumatise him. As we stood around, I noticed that Craig's Bible was lying open on the table.

"Have you been reading to him?" I whispered to Winnie, and she nodded.

When I got closer, I saw that the Bible was opened at Psalm 91.

"Psalm 91?" I asked. She nodded again.

Through all the drama, my lips engaged a smile.

"My daughter Debbie too," I told her. Winnie and I touched hands and smiled together.

When Sister Debbie had finished administering the medication, she asked if she could pray with the family. She anointed our son with oil, and prayed for all of us. I asked her if she thought she would see Craig alive again, and she said she didn't think so. Characteristically, Craig proved everyone wrong.

He had a reasonable night, but Ian and I didn't. I suppose you could say Craig was in a type of coma, probably induced by the medication. He was never to come out of it. I made up my mind that I wouldn't leave the house again as long as he was still alive. Tuesday came and his agitation worsened, so Sister Debbie increased the dose of morphine, adding Dormicum to sedate him and Serenace to prevent nausea and anxiety. Tracy came to say goodbye, but she didn't stay long, and I didn't want any other visitors. I lay on the bed with my boy for a long time in the morning. I needed to be close to him. He didn't seem to know, but I like to think that perhaps he did. A few people phoned to ask if they could come to see us, but I said no, and they respected that. I wanted to be alone with my son. A little later, Winnie and I were with him when he suddenly spewed up a lot of dark green muck that looked like old motor oil. I got a dreadful fright. I'd never seen anything like that. Again, I thought he was about to die. His breathing was still very irregular, but he continued to live. I phoned Ian, telling him I thought he should come home, which he did. Lindy had a bad dose of flu, but she paid us a long visit in the afternoon. She was there when Pastor André came to pray with us. I'm very grateful for Pastor André and his church, who have been praying for us for some months.

Ian decided to stay off work, and on Wednesday Craig appeared to be in pain, so the morphine was again increased. Sister Debbie came every day, and every day became tougher. Lindy was there too. When Edith came, she spent a few minutes alone with Craig. She needed to say her own personal goodbye. I think it gave her a degree of closure to the long road we'd walked together. From here on we would remember our children fondly, believing that they would meet at last. They had a lot in common, and perhaps it is now time for them to hold hands, as their mothers did. We'd like to think so. We hadn't seen Georgie for over two months, but I phoned her, and she arrived with two of her daughters.

Brian was leaving for the States that evening and he came to say goodbye. No words can describe my anguish, knowing that in that room my youngest boy was bidding farewell to his brother for the last time on this earth, and Craig wasn't even able to respond. My stomach was tied into a million knots that no human being would ever be capable of untying. There could only be one thing worse than this, and that was death itself.

Doug arrived after work, and he and Lindy spent some time with us. We thought about Brian on that aircraft, and we wondered how he was dealing with his sorrow.

Thursday went by with little change. Lindy and Nicky came to support us. Craig's mouth was very dry, so we put a bit of ice on his lips, although it made no difference. He hadn't had any water for four days. His hands were sweaty, but I held on to them whenever I could.

Is there any point to anything? I asked myself. It all seemed futile, but it wasn't really. There was a divine plan, there had to be.

During the day I was talking to Lindy about who could fill the role of the fourth pallbearer at the funeral in Brian's absence, because now we had only Ian, Doug and Tony. I casually mentioned that it was a shame their old friend Douglas was now living in the UK.

"Oh but I saw on Facebook that he and Belinda are here on holiday," Lindy told me.

I was amazed and soon got in touch with them. They came to visit Craig, and Douglas agreed to do the honours at the memorial service. What a shock this was for them. They had come to South Africa for their brother's wedding, but would first have to attend a funeral; but God does work in mysterious ways. Craig had told me that he had two brothers called Doug, and now these two so-called brothers would be escorting him on his final journey on this earth. We were all very sad that Brian could not be there, but we knew that he would grateful that his dear friend Douglas was there for Craig, in place of him. A few months later, we were to appreciate the importance of Brian's trip to the States. He was to become one of only about a hundred people in the world, and the first one in Africa to attain the Microsoft Certified Master—SharePoint 2010 certification. Ian and I did not know then, that we would soon be celebrating our littlest boy, who almost exactly four years ago had peddled his bicycle in a one hundred kilometer race for his brother. God had orchestrated His plan with absolute precision.

On Thursday evening, 2 August, I was helping Ian change Craig's nappy, when the sight of his skeletal body annihilated my mind. His protruding hip bones were so horrific, that I found myself holding on to the door handle, to save myself from falling over, as I broke down in torrential tears. I abandoned Ian and went tearing into the lounge, bellowing at the top of my voice. My poor husband didn't know what to do. I was in a state of collapse, and he was trying to deal with our dying son at the same time. He dropped everything, and came running after me.

"Stop it," he cried, "Craig can hear you! You're upsetting him!"

Was that true? Could he hear me? I still don't know, but it did stop my hysteria. Someone later said that my outburst was a normal reaction to the current state of affairs. I pondered over whether to write this, but I want people to know that even though watching a loved one slowly die is excruciatingly painful, they are not alone; it is possible to bear the grief, and it does get easier.

Friday, 3 August 2012

Merriam is standing in for Winnie this weekend. Things are very bad. He could go any minute. We all thought he would go three days ago, but he's still hanging on. It's now five days without food or water. This man has a huge constitution.

As is customary when Merriam comes, she begins her morning by singing to her patient. This morning she was singing "Let Your Living Water Flow", when I walked into the room. Halfway through the song, I joined with her, and we sang together. For sure, our tears were mingling. I could swear Craig has smiled a few times today, but like a tiny baby, one cannot be sure if it's a real smile, or just wind. Either way, I haven't seen him smile for months, so it was good. He's very peaceful now. Merriam told me that last week he said there was an aeroplane parked right in front of him. I sat on his bed and made up a little story about that aeroplane. I told him that he should board now, because it was time for him to go. I said he should hurry, or he might miss the flight. Then I talked him through the walk to the aircraft, telling him to sit down, and fasten his seat belt.

"Look," I told him, "There's Jesus sitting beside you. And there are angels on both wings. Can you see them?"

His silence saddened me.

"Craigie, I'm waving goodbye," I whispered, fighting the tears that blurred my vision, "It's all up to the Pilot now."

A little while later Doug phoned, and when I told him that story, he said I should tell Craig to switch off his cell phone on the aircraft; so I did, and that made me smile.

I told Merriam not to come the next day, because she was traumatised. Ian and I would be able to manage alone. We were not aware then that she was to sing that same beautiful song as a tribute to our son at his funeral.

Chapter 27

Sunday, 5 August 2012—Email to friends around the world

Dear Friends

It is with great sadness that we have to tell you that Craig passed away yesterday evening, 4 August 2012, three months before his forty-first birthday. His journey was a long and difficult one, but he left peacefully, and we know that his faith and courage over the past four years has touched many lives. Never once did we hear him complain, or ask "why me," and his biggest concern during his painful ordeal was about how his family would be able to deal with it. We will be eternally grateful for the blessing of our wonderful son, who was the bravest man we have ever known.

Thanks to all those who have prayed and walked this road with us, many of whom live on the other side of the world, and we have never had the pleasure of meeting face to face; but your hearts have become one with ours. The support from friends and family has been overwhelming.

To God be the Glory.

With much love

Ian and Léonie

Ian and I were in the house, but not with him, when he passed away, early in the evening. We found him looking serene, as if he had left quietly and without pain. For the purpose of this book, I have chosen not to describe our grief, but to keep it to the confines of our close friends and family. I can only say that there is no pain like that of losing a child, no matter what the circumstances.

Two days after he passed away I received an email from a lady called Jo, whom we have not met, but who has been following Craig's illness through emails. She told me that she'd had a vision. She seemed to be in the back a small aeroplane. Craig got in next to the pilot, who turned to him and said, "Ready for take-off?' and Craig replied, "Yes, sir." The pilot turned his face towards Craig, and Jo knew that it was the Lord. As they were coming in to land, she saw rows and rows of angels, but did not experience the flight, nor the landing. "You can be assured," she told me, "that your precious son is with our Lord."

Was that not confirmation of the aeroplane that Craig told Merriam was standing in front of him? Was that not confirmation of the account I gave him about boarding the aircraft, and waiting for the Pilot to take off? Who knows? But what I am confident of is that he's safe in the arms of Jesus.

The day before the funeral, I was once again sitting in our sun lounge, looking out of those big windows, meditating on how, a few months ago, I had written that this would surely be the winter of our lives, and surely it has been. In affirmation of that, it was snowing outside. Snow rarely falls in this part of the world. A soft white blanket covered the ground, and the big leafless tree was tinged with spots of crisp snow-flakes. On its branches sat the doves, none the worse for the weather. I was contemplating that if God looks after the birds of the air, how much more He cares for us. The birds have no worries at all, so why should we, who have learned to trust in Him? I smiled, just a little, and I thanked Him for loving my son so much that He took him home, away from the troubles of this world. Very soon spring would be here. New leaves would begin to sprout on that tree, and almost before we had time to bid Jack Frost adieu, the doves would be hidden from view. Just as the seasons come and go, God promised that our days of mourning would end. Outside the snow was already beginning to melt. The doves were calling to one another, and a brightly coloured crested barbet dared to land in the bird bath. Two grey louries perched on the top of a nearby tree, and in some hidden place a shy Burchell's coucal could be heard. I couldn't see any of our resident raucous hadedas, but they'd be back, they always are.

The house was strangely quiet. I turned my eyes inwards to the beautiful flowers that adorned the room, reminding me once again of our precious son. I had told him many times about the place he was going to, but I have no doubt that my description did not come close to the real thing. As I considered the seasons of our lives, I recalled something I'd written many years ago.

> Heaven is a place where summer is forever, where the shades of autumn blend in with the viridity of spring and winter is but a graceful picture of a nameless lady in white.

If a funeral can be beautiful, then Craig's was. Many people commented that it didn't seem like a funeral at all, and one person remarked that it was the first memorial service she'd ever been to where she felt certain that the deceased person was really in Heaven. Craig loved the Lord with all his heart, and knowing that is what sustained us throughout his long ordeal.

We know where he is now, and that assurance is invaluable. We thank God for a son and brother, whose loving and giving heart will remain one with ours for the rest of our days. He fought a brave and difficult battle, yet never questioned his affliction. His legacy will live on in the hearts of many people.

Conclusion

If I've learned anything from this experience, it's that God can take the greatest tragedy, and turn it into the greatest testimony. I have never believed that God caused our son to have a brain tumour. That is the devil's work. Does that mean the devil won the battle? Absolutely not! Yes, God could have eliminated that evil tumour right at the start of it, but He didn't. We could go round and round in circles asking why, and God would probably not answer us, because we would probably not be able to comprehend His reasoning. He is God Almighty. His wisdom is way, way above anything we could ever imagine.

I choose to believe that God has used Craig's infirmity to draw people closer to Him. He has shown His glory in every miracle that He performed during Craig's seemingly long battle with cancer. Craig grew much closer to Him in his latter years than he had ever been before. The devil strove to destroy him, but in the end, God was victorious. Many were witness to Craig's faith and courage. He even wrote on Facebook, after he was diagnosed, that he had huge faith in God.

Many times I've considered how Mary and the disciples must have felt as they watched their beloved Jesus suffering on that awful cross. During the past few years, I have often tried to put myself in Mary's place, imagining how she must have cried out to God, the very Father of her Son, how she must have wrangled between her emotions and her knowledge that the Father knew what He was doing. Her distress as she watched her Son's anguish, both physical and mental, would have been indescribable. She was His mother. She carried Him in her womb, fed Him at her breast, weaned Him, nurtured Him, and stood by His side all the days of His earthly life. But it didn't stop there. She is still standing by Him, and that is where I draw my strength from. Because of what He did at Calvary, her Son never left her side, just as He has never left my side. And one day, my own son, Craig Ian Edwards, will stand by my side again, in Heaven.

IN LOVING MEMORY

OF

CRAIG IAN EDWARDS

30 October 1971-4 August 2012

TO MY SON

Will the ache in my heart ever leave me?
Will the tear in my eye ever go?
Will the shadows that fall in the evening
Ever turn into light rays and glow?
I'm numbed by the sound of his music,
I'm crushed by the visions I see;
I can't walk through the day without wishing
He was walking that pathway with me.
And yet shall I smile at the children,
Who run through the puddles at play;
I'll sing with the birds in the morning,
And dance when the blue skies turn grey.
I'll pray for the sick and the dying—
Hold hands with the ones left behind;
And I'll laugh when the sound of his laughter
Rings out from the voice in my mind.

Lightning Source UK Ltd.
Milton Keynes UK
UKOW041654080513

210378UK00002B/33/P

9 781481 780919